Picture Within A Picture

An Illustrated Guide
to the Origins of Chinese Characters

Written by Shi Zhengyu

NEW WORLD PRESS   BEIJING, CHINA

First Edition 1997
Second Printing 1999

Edited by Meng Fanling
Book design by Fang Wei

ISBN 7-80005-332-6

Published by
NEW WORLD PRESS
24 Baiwanzhuang Road, Beijing, 100037, China

Distributed by
NEW WORLD PRESS
24 Baiwanzhuang Road, Beijing, 100037, China

Printed in the People's Republic of China

CONTENTS

PREFACE

It is a pleasure for me to write, as requested, a preface to the English edition of *Picture Within A Picture: An Illustrated Guide to the Origins of Chinese Characters*, written by Shi Zhengyu. I do wish to avail myself on this occasion to write a few words on this interesting book full of historical background events and knowledge, along with ancient forms of Chinese characters and picture illustrations. This work reveals her arduous pursuit and naive curiosity to trace the origins and evolution of Chinese characters. Having read through the book, I believe that other readers of the book will find the characters lovely and interesting. I am grateful to her for her kind request. The book is characterized by the interesting and delightful as well as the scientific manner in which it is written. I will focus my comments on the latter.

Ancient Chinese characters are a large accumulation of pictographic characters. In other words, they express their meanings by resemblance to other objects. The characters, either single or ones in combination, have been readjusted and standardized since the Qin Dynasty, and have evolved into today's characters. These characters have been the carriers of the Chinese language during its long historical development and inherited the meanings and pronunciations from their ancient counterparts. Now, the character "日 (sun)" no longer looks like the sun; "眼 (eye)" does not look like the eye; "水 (water)" does not show ripples; "要 (want)" does not resemble a man with hands on the waist; ···However, they not only can record the basic elements of the Chinese language, but also structure the sound theory of other words with their own pronunciation and meanings. Pictographic characters unify form and meaning. The unity, representing a historical concept, has been accepted universally in the long historical development. The marriage of form and meaning is an inevitable outcome of history, not depending on anyone's will. For this reason, form and meaning cannot be interpreted freely; or in other words, interpretation must be well-grounded and in conformity with form and theory. Conformity with form means conformity with the form undergoing historical evolution; conformity

i

with theory means conformity with the theory agreed upon during historical development. Modern Chinese characters may sometimes seem to contradict each other. After tracing back their historical evolution, conformity with form and theory appears more clearly and is understandable.

In addition to the opinions referred to above, free interpretation is not admissible because all characters are systematized. Not one of them stands alone by itself. They became interconnected with historical evolution. One character being wrongly interpreted, will cause troubles to the interpretation of interrelated characters. An example can be cited pertaining to the interpretation of the character "弛(limp)". According to an interpretation, as the component "弓(bow)" resembles a snake, and so the character means "松弛 (limp)". Such an interpretation does not take into consideration the fact that characters, incorporating the component "弓", as in "张" and "引" carry the opposite meaning of "松弛", while characters as "弹", "弥" have nothing to do with the meaning of "松弛". Consequently, how can other characters be construed if "弛" is interpreted in such a sense?

Good interpretation requires first of all the understanding of the rules for structuring characters, and secondly, the mastering of an overall system of characters, and thirdly, the knowledge of the historical evolution of structuring characters. It may be said that it is too troublesome. It is true that it is not an easy job to improve cultural quality, however, it is not advisable to, for the sake of simplicity, neglect scientific rules. In the end, it will cause much more troubles. Following the rules and using a correct approach, work can be accomplished naturally with much convenience.

The objective of the book designed by the author is to discover a scientific rule for teaching Chinese characters. For this end, she began with ancient characters, leading people to an understanding of history of the evolution of Chinese characters. She has selected single characters as fundamental units. Each by itself acts as an independent character. They are then supplemented with some ancient ones containing more than one unit. By using these fundamental units capable of forming other characters, she masters the key links for a systematized structure of Chinese characters and this is the starting point for learning Chinese characters. Ancient forms of these single characters happen to be pictographic characters, which gives birth to the idea that picture illustrations provide resemblance of the characters to the objects and can be conducive to the understanding of the initial theory on structuring characters. This is of great help to beginners, both children and foreigners. What is more important is that by applying the accomplishments of research in ancient characters, she endeavors to interpret the forms and meanings of characters in conformity to historical events and the overall structuring system, avoiding arbitrary interpretations. Despite what remains open to discussion or that interpretation of some characters can be improved, I submit that she is particular about the choices among many opinions pertaining to the interpretation as to what should be used or rejected and no free guesses have been made as others have done. She speaks of the original meaning, the extended meaning or the meaning used today; she has paid due attention to linking traditional characters with simplified ones. She has not neglected the pronunciation attached to silent characters. It is obvious that she tries to popularize ancient characters through the study of modern Chinese. I believe that her objective represents serious pursuance and implied wisdom which will bring nothing but success.

In the absence of reference books for teachers teaching Chinese characters in elementary and secondary schools and for foreigners learning them, *Picture Within A Picture: An Illustrated Guide to the Origins of Chinese Characters*, is a good book for reference and for this reason, serious study and improvements need to be made in respect of the questions pertaining to the selection and interpretation of the characters as well as the picture illustrations and editing. Popularization of science is under way now and for popularization, scientific attitude is absolutely needed. Otherwise, people will be affected adversely. A good book with good objectives needs to be revised and perfected again and again and I believe that with the continued efforts of the author and her cooperators, *Picture Within A Picture: An Illustrated Guide to the Origins of Chinese Characters* will become a master work and be greeted with the appreciation of more and more readers.

Wang Ning
Beijing Normal University
February 28, 1996

Wang Ning
Beijing Normal University
February 28, 2008

SECTION ONE

HUMAN BEINGS

rén

人

Ancient Chinese formed the character "人" from the sideview of a standing person. When used as a component of another character, it appears written as "亻", indicating an object or action relating to people.

It was said in *The Narration and Explanation of Characters*, the first dictionary compiled by Xu Shen to interpret the meaning of Chinese characters in a comprehensive and systematic manner, that people were "the most precious thing in the world", or the most respected in the world. This shows the naive humanism of ancient China.

cóng

从 　　The shape of this character shows two people walking together, indicating one person following another. Therefore, one who
follows another is also called "随从(suícóng: entourage, atten-
dant)". Because this character shows two people, it has also come to
mean to gather or assemble. The traditional character "叢" refers to a
gathering or body of plants, such as small trees or bushes. Thus, it has
been simplified as "丛". Comprising this character is a "一" which, as a
self-explanatory character, here has no significance. "从" indicates the
pronunciation, as well as expresses the meaning. For example, plants
and trees growing together are referred to as "树丛(shùcóng)" or "草丛
(cǎocóng)", etc.

　　In the period of the Three Kingdoms, Cao Cao used the following
lines of poetry to express the vitality of the natural landscape: "Gathering
together trees are growing, flourishing various plants are seeming."

4

bǐ
比
In ancient Chinese, this character is a sideview of two people standing. The difference between "比" and "从(cóng)" is that the figures are facing opposite directions: in "从", they face to the left, in "比", to the right.

"比" shows two people close to each other, indicating intimacy. Lines of classic Chinese poetry say that "海内存知己，天涯若比邻(Intimate friends are found elsewhere in the country, remote areas appear to be next-door neighbors)" and "在天愿作比翼鸟,在地愿为连理枝(In the sky, we'd be two love-birds to fly wing to wing, on the earth, two trees with branches twined from spring to spring)". "比" in the quoted lines means "close to".

On the ocean bottom lives the flounder, or flatfish, whose eyes move closer together as the fish grows, eventually migrating entirely to one side of the head. We call this fish "比目鱼(bǐmùyú)".

běi

北

Two people sitting back to back forms "北". Later, "北" came to indicate a direction, north. Its original meaning is expressed by adding a "月（肉）(indicating flesh)" underneath, thus becoming "背", meaning "back". The pronunciation changes as well (from the third to the fourth tone as "bèi").

In a battle, when the losing side turns and retreats, it is called "败北(bàiběi)" (the pronunciation remains in the third tone).

丽 lì   The ancient Chinese character shows two people walking next to each other, meaning to form a couple or a pair. Later, a "亻" was added to make "俪", found in "伉俪 (kànglì)", meaning a husband and a wife, which was the original meaning of "丽".

Later, "丽" plus "鹿 (lù: deer)" made "麗", signifying a deer with a magnificent coat, and meaning "美丽 (měilì: beautiful)", or "华丽 (huálì: magnificent, resplendent)". It has been simplified back to "丽", but no longer carries the original meaning of two persons walking side by side.

7

zhòng

众

The ancient form of this character shows three people laboring under the sun. In ancient script, "三 (sān: three)" was often a nominal way of signifying a great number. Because there are always a lot of people plowing, this character means "multitudinous" or "numerous".

In traditional characters, this character was standardized as "衆"; in simplified form, it is "众", meaning "three people make a crowd".

huà In ancient script, this character depicts one
化 person standing upright and one person upside-
down. Because there can be no greater change
than a complete reversal of something, this character
came to mean "change".

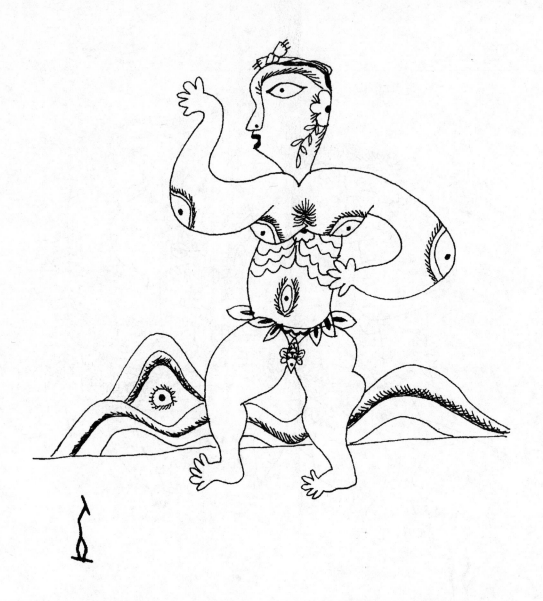

tǐng

挺

The ancient form of this character shows a sideview of a man standing in an upright position, with arms up and chest out.

The character had been standardized as "壬", the ancient form of today's "挺".

The difference between "壬(tǐng)" and "壬(rén)" is that the middle horizontal stroke of "壬" is short, whereas that of "壬" is longer.

dòu

斗

The ancient form of this character resembles two people fighting, with their hair bristling due to anger.

The traditional character appears as "鬥", and has been simplified to "斗". The simplified character is the same as that for a kind of container used to measure grain, but the two are pronounced differently. The "斗" which means to fight is pronounced in the fourth tone, whereas when used as a measurement, it is read in the third tone.

qiān

千   The ancient form of this character is of the sideview of a person, with a line drawn across the body, indicating a number of one thousand; drawing two lines indicates two thousand.

There is a verse in the first collection of poems in ancient China, *The Book of Songs*, which reads "十千维耦 (shí qiān wéi ǒu: describing a scene of 10,000 people plowing side by side)". Here, "千" takes on the meaning of one thousand.

shī   In ancient times, "尸" was a person who played the role of
尸   dead ancestors, receiving offerings during ancestor worship
    rites. Because he represented one who had already passed
away, the character "尸" shows a person who is sitting and cannot
move. Later, "死 (sǐ: death)" was added to make "屍", meaning a
corpse.

ér

儿 In ancient script, this character depicts the soft, yielding head of a newborn child, thus meaning "婴儿 (yīng'ér: infant)". The traditional form of the character was written "兒", and has been simplified to "儿".

"儿" as a variant of "人" comprises other characters as in "先 (xiān)" "允 (yǔn)" "光 (guāng)", etc.

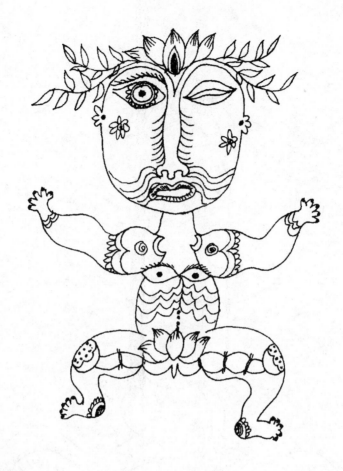

tiān
天 The ancient form of this character depicts a frontal view of a person with an enlarged head, and signifies the crown of the head. Today, the top portion of the skulls of a person or some animals is called "天灵盖 (tiānlínggài: the crown of the head)", and a type of Chinese medicine for treating headaches is called "正天丸 (zhèngtiānwán: pill of Chinese medicine for headache)", hinting at the original imaginary connection of the sky with the head.

Later, the vast space over one's head containing the sun, the moon, and the stars came to be called "天空 (tiānkōng: sky)".

yuán

元

This character originally represented a sideview of the protruding head of a person standing; thus, its o-riginal meaning was "head". Later, this came to mean "originator", "first", and "occupying the first place". For example, the highest scorer on an imperial examination is called "状元(zhuàng·yuan)", the first day of a new year is called "元旦(yuándàn)", the highest leader of a country is called "元首(yuánshǒu:head of the state)", and a doer of atrocious crimes is called "元凶(yuánxiōng)".

16

jiè

介

The ancient form of this character resembles an ancient warrior clad in armor. Ancient armor was made of small pieces of leather sewn together, which are represented in the ancient character by the small, dot-like strokes. Because armor is, of course, hard, the shell of a beetle is called "介壳 (jièqiào)", and a scab on a person's skin is called a "疥疮 (jièchuāng)" (the radical "疒" indicates something to do with diseases or illness).

xiōng   The ancient form of this character is of a per-
兄   son kneeling on the ground, head upraised,
mouth open. The open mouth signifies one who
is issuing orders or praying to the gods, so the original
meaning of this character related to the mouth and to an
elder. From this, we get "兄", a respectful term of address for an elder person.

zhǎng

长

The ancient form of this character depicts a man with long hair grasping a walking stick, as found in "长老（zhǎnglǎo）", meaning "elder". Because the elderly have lived longer than others, this character is also pronounced "cháng", as in "长久 (chángjiǔ)", meaning "a long time".

The traditional form of this character appears as "長", and, written in regular script instead of running handwriting, the character has been simplified to "长".

lǎo

老

In ancient script, this character depicts a man with a bent back, leaning on a stick, and with long hair, expressing "of great age".

kǎo In ancient Chinese, "考", too, shows a man bent over 考 with age, with long hair, clutching a stick, meaning "old". In general, it is used to indicate one's deceased father, as in "如丧考妣(rú sàng kǎo bǐ: '妣' means one's deceased mother)".

In modern Chinese, "考" can mean "to test", "to examine", or "to ascertain". These later meanings are all derived from phonetic loan characters, or homophonic words.

bǎo
保
This character shows a person holding a small child. Therefore, it means "保护（bǎohù）", to protect, or "保全（bǎoquán）", to maintain. From this, a cloth used to wrap an infant to protect it from wind and cold is called a "襁褓（qiǎngbǎo）" (the radical "衤" indicates something to do with cloth). A strong building meant to defend a strategic point is a "堡垒（bǎolěi）" ("土" indicates a structure made of earth or stones).

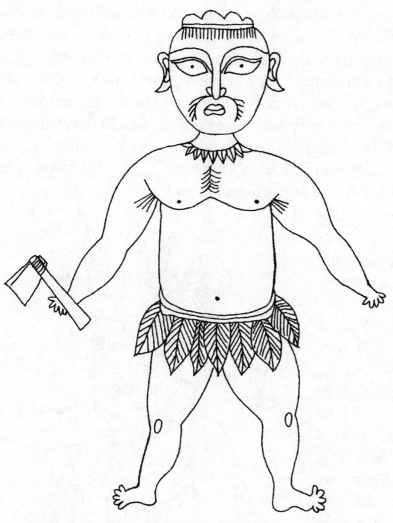

大
dà
    This character, in ancient script, shows a man standing with arms and legs outstretched, as if to exaggerate "how great man is" and later means "big" by extension as in "大小(dàxiǎo：big and small)".

wáng

王

This character, in ancient script, shows a huge man and means leader. Some scholars held it represented an axe, an ancient weapon, signifying conquerors.

"王" was termed a monarch in the pre-Qin times, such as Zhou Wen Wang, Zhou Wu Wang known as enlightened monarchs and Zhou Wang as a tyrant. During the fall of the Zhou Dynasty various states might have had its own "王(monarchs)", for example, the Dukes of Chu, Wu, Yue states, etc. Since the Qin Dynasty "王" has been the highest lordship conferred to officials by emperors. For example, "诸侯王(zhūhóuwáng: the dukes)", "藩王(fānwáng: military governors for prefectures in charge of army, politics, civil administration, finance)", "郡王(jùnwáng: prefectural governor)", "亲王(qīnwáng: princes)", etc.

In the process of history, various nationalities worshipped and praised heroes and heroines. It is said in *The Book of Songs, Section Xiao Ya, Northern Mountains*: "溥天之下，莫非王土。率土之滨，莫非王臣。(There is no land under the vast heaven that does not belong to the emperor. There are no subjects on the vast land who do not belong to the emperor.)" Such was the emperors' ideal life of expanding territory and dominating the whole country.

"Wang" is one of the most popular surnames in today's China.

lì In ancient script, this character represents the figure of a man standing upright, with the bottom line indicating the ground.

bìng
并

The ancient form of this character resembles two people standing by each other, and therefore means "next to", or "simultaneously". Some modern phrases, such as "并肩作战（bìng jiān zuò zhàn: to fight side by side)", and "齐头并进（qí tóu bìng jìn: to advance side by side)" still carry this meaning. Two lotus flowers growing off the same stalk is termed "并蒂莲（bìngdìlián)", and is often used in literature to describe a married couple who are passionately in love.

The traditional form is "並", and has been shortened to "并". As a consonant, "并" is only retained in the Chinese character "碰（pèng)".

jìng

竞 The character resembles two men side by side with head ornaments. In ancient script two men following one after another means chase and competition by extension.

The character is standardized as "競" and simplified as "竞".

shì

This character is of a person standing, but with the legs drawn together. Young men in ancient times, once they reached the age of marriage, were termed "士".

The bottom horizontal stroke of this character is shorter than the upper horizontal stroke, thus distinguishing it from "土(tǔ)", meaning "earth".

28

jiāo 交 The ancient form of this character is a "大" (the front view of a person), crossing his legs. Therefore, its original meaning is literally "to cross", "to intertwine".

fū
夫   This character is a front view of an adult man (as in "大"), wearing his hair bundled on top of his head, and fastened with pin; it is the image of a "manly man".

jiā

夹

In ancient script, this character depicts a man ("大"), gripped by two people under his arms. Thus, by applying force from different directions, the object in the middle is fixed firmly in place. For example, candies with fruits or other edibles inside them are called "夹心糖(jiāxīntáng)". A river flowing between two mountains or hills is called a "峡(xiá)" ("山" indicates that high protrusions of earth rise out of the water on both sides).

The traditional form of this character is written "夾".

yāng   The ancient form of this character resembles a man
央   ("大") framed by a doorway. Therefore, the literal meaning of this character is "央(central)". Today, the shape of
a doorway has evolved into "凵", while the form of the person
still appears as "大".

kàng The character in ancient script pro-
兀 trudes the neck and so is the meaning.

yì

亦

The ancient form of this character shows a man with arms and legs outstretched, with two dots indicating his armpits. Later, "亦" was appropriated to mean "也(yě：also or too)", and another character "腋(yè)" was created to mean "armpit". In that character, "月(肉)" indicates that the word has something to do with the human body, while "夜(yè)" represents the pronunciation.

zǐ

子   This character, in ancient script, represents a small child wrapped in swaddling clothes, and originally carries the meaning of an infant boy or girl. However, today it specifically refers to boys.

Because boys traditionally had higher positions than girls, "子" therefore is also a manner of respectful address. For example, in "子曰诗云(zǐ yuē shī yún)" and "诸子百家(zhū zǐ bǎi jiā)", "子" refers to a man of high learning as in "孔子(Confucius)", "老子(Lao Zi)", "庄子(Zhuang Zi)", etc.

xiào

孝 The ancient form of this character is constructed from a "老 (lǎo: old)" (later reduced to just "耂") and a "子", which, when put together, means to take care of the elderly, or to show filial obedience to one's parents.

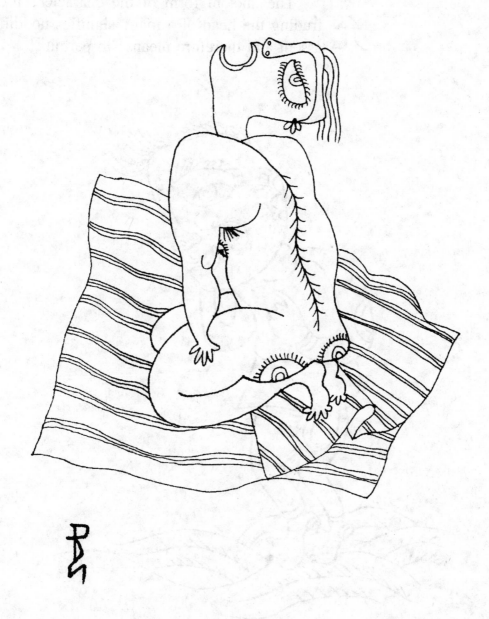

qiàn

欠

This character represents a man yawning with a wide open mouth. A yawn shows that someone is lacking energy, and therefore, "欠" means "欠缺 (qiànquē: deficiency)".

yŭn

允

The ancient form of the character, protruding the head of a man, signifies nodding assent and therefore means "to permit".

chán

孱 This character resembles a dead person ("尸[屍]") leaving behind many children. Thus, this character means "frail", or "weak", as in "孱弱(chánruò)".

Here, the depiction of three "子" doesn't literally mean three children, but simply indicates "a lot".

yùn
孕   This character depicts a woman with a protruding belly, that of a pregnant woman. In the standard modern form of this character "孕", "乃(nǎi)" is a variant of "人(rén:person)".

xiào

肖

The ancient form of this character depicts a newborn infant covered in bloody fluid, indicating blood ties. Through the significance of a blood connection, this word acquires the meanings of "similar", or "to resemble". Therefore, for example, a portrait painting of someone is called a "肖像（xiàoxiàng）"; something that has been drawn or sketched in extremely true to life detail is described as "惟妙惟肖（wéi miào wéi xiào）"; and descendants who don't carry on the undertakings of their ancestors are known as "不肖子孙（bù xiào zǐ sūn）".

In the modern script, this character is written as "肖", "月（肉）" indicates a blood kinship.

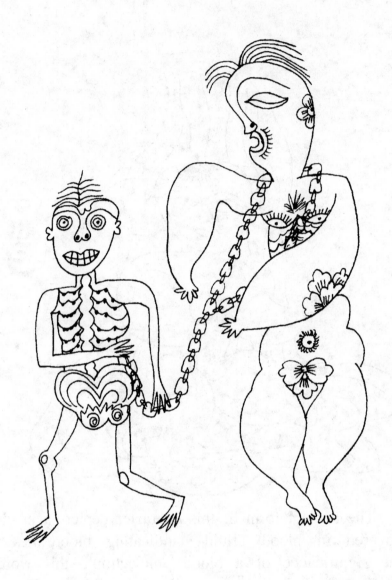

sǐ   This character consists of the components "人" and "歹".

死 "歹" is pronounced "niè", and indicates bones, or a dead person. Therefore, the ancient form of this character is of a person, head bowed and offering condolences to a dead person, and means "死亡(sǐwáng:death)".

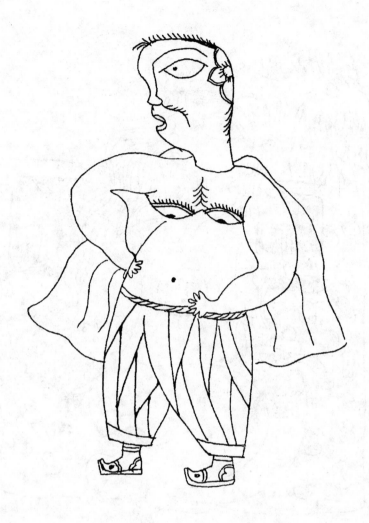

shēn
身
The ancient form of this character shows the sideview of a man with a large potbelly—an image of someone who is held in high regard among others. This character can be found in the modern word for "身分 (shēnfèn : identity)". Because it depicts a big belly, it has also come to describe a pregnant woman, as in "身孕 (shēnyùn)".

In *jiaguwen* (inscriptions on bones and tortoise shells), "身" and "孕" are the same character.

女　nǚ　　In ancient script this character depicts a person kneeling, with hands either crossed in front or tied behind the back, representing an abducted woman. This reflects the forced marriage customs of antiquity.

This character may also be interpreted as the form of a woman sitting, expressing the social practices of a matriarchal society in which the women remain in one place while the men go out to other tribes.

hǎo

好

This character depicts a woman cradling an infant child. In the Shang Dynasty, "好" was a surname, so the "女" component is a vestige of a matrilineal society. A child in its mother's bosom is extraordinarily fortunate and therefore this character is adopted to mean "good".

mǔ

母

This character originally represented a woman with two protruding breasts, indicating a woman nurturing a child, and hence, a mother. Because a mother has the most authority over her child, especially in a matriarchal society, "母" has also been used to mean "no" or "not". This extension in meaning led to a slight alteration in the character in order to distinguish the two meanings. The form meaning "no" came to be written as "毋", pronounced "wú".

46

rǔ

乳

The ancient form of this character represents a mother nursing a child in her arms, thus meaning "哺乳(bǔrǔ: to breast-feed)".

ruò

若 This character originally depicted a woman combing her hair, meaning "gentle" or "meek". While in modern Japanese, this character has retained this meaning, in China, it has evolved into a function word meaning "if", "to seem", or "to be like".

hòu

后

In ancient script, this character shows a woman giving birth to a child. When the fetus emerges, it comes head first, and so part of the character is a "子" written upside-down.

"后" was used in ancient times in the titles of emperors or kings, as in "后稷(hòujì:the minister of agriculture under Emperor Shun, also regarded as the god of agriculture)". This practice is a vestige of a matriarchal society. Today "后" takes on the meaning of "後(later or after)" by simplification.

Later "后" also came to be used in referring to the wife of an emperor, as in "皇后 (huánghòu)", meaning "empress", and "后妃 (hòufēi)", meaning "concubine".

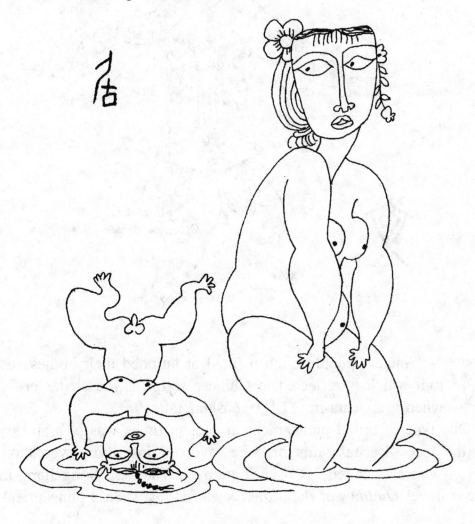

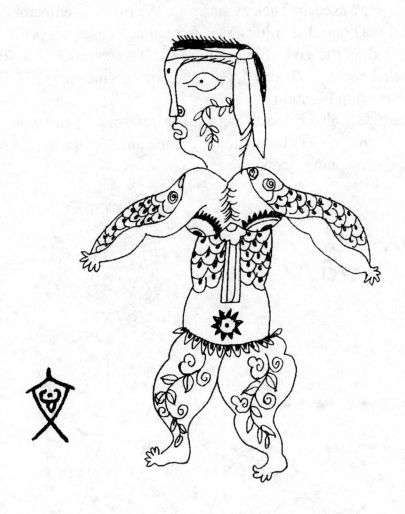

wén
文

Ancient people often painted or tattooed their bodies, a custom which is reflected in Chinese script as the character "文", when it appears in "文身(wénshēn：tattoo)".

One type of brutal punishment in ancient times was to brand or tattoo the face. Because this practice involved inscribing words on the face, it was also called "文面(wénmiàn)". The hero Song Jiang in the classic novel *Outlaws of the Marsh* suffered just such a punishment.

kè
克
The ancient form of this character resembles a man wearing a helmet, with both hands planted firmly on his waist, as in the pose of a brave warrior. Thus, the original meaning of "克" was "to be equal to (doing a task)", or "able". For instance, the phrase "攻克(gōngkè)" can mean to capture an enemy in battle or to overcome difficulty. A laborer who is both diligent and frugal is described by the phrase "克勤克俭(kè qín kè jiǎn)".

shǒu

首

As this character resembles a head in ancient script, its original meaning is just that: head. For example, a head chopped off in battle is called "首级（shǒují）", and when one cannot bear to recall or look back upon some past event, it is called "不堪回首（bù kān huí shǒu）". Later, meanings such as "highest", "leading", and "first" were born out of this original sense. For instance, the highest office in a monarchical cabinet is the prime minister, or "首相（shǒuxiàng）"; to bear the brunt of an attack or a disaster is termed "首当其冲（shǒu dāng qí chōng）"; and the person who bears the most responsibility or guilt for a disaster or crime is called "罪魁祸首（zuì kuí huò shǒu）", meaning "the chief culprit".

yè

页　　The ancient form of this character exaggerates the head of a person. Thus, the original meaning of "页" was "head". Later it came to be used to mean "页(page of a book, etc.)". By itself it no longer meant "head". However, as a component in other characters, such as "颊(jiá)", "颜(yán)", "额(é)", "颅(lú)", and "顽(wán)", it indicates something to do with the "head".

The traditional form of the character is written as "頁".

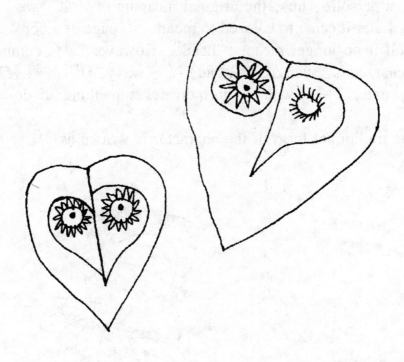

xīn

心

In ancient script, "心" is a representation of the heart. As a component of other characters, it indicates something to do with people's emotions or psychology. It may appear as "心" in the middle or at the bottom of a character, as in "慶（qìng：celebration）"or "慈（cí：kindness）"; in the left of a character, as "忄", as in "性（xìng）" or "情（qíng）"; or as "小", again at the bottom of a character, like in "慕（mù）".

máo

毛　　This character represents eyebrows, facial hair, or the hair of beasts. Ancient Chinese writing utensils were fashioned out of bamboo and the hairs of sheep, weasels, and other animals. The modern simplified character for "pen" consists of "毛" and "⺮ (meaning 'bamboo')", resulting in "笔" (bǐ: written as "筆" in the traditional form). "笔" later came to refer to any sort of writing utensil: those still made with hairs are called "毛笔(máobǐ)", while others, such as "铅笔 (qiānbǐ: pencil)", "钢笔(gāngbǐ: pen)", and "粉笔(fěnbǐ: chalk)" have nothing whatever to do with hair.

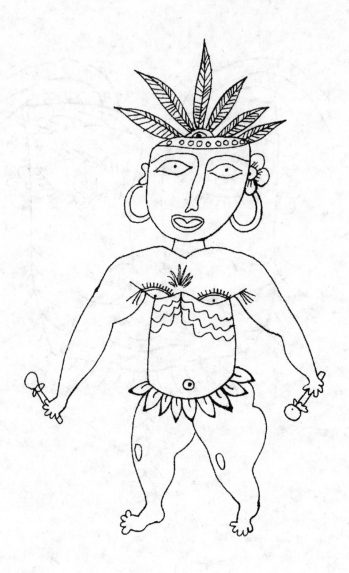

měi
美　　　This character depicts a person（indicated by "大"）with his head decorated with feathers, meaning "美丽（měilì：beautiful）".

mù   The ancient form of this character is a drawing
目   of an eye. Later, it came to be written vertically
     instead of horizontally.

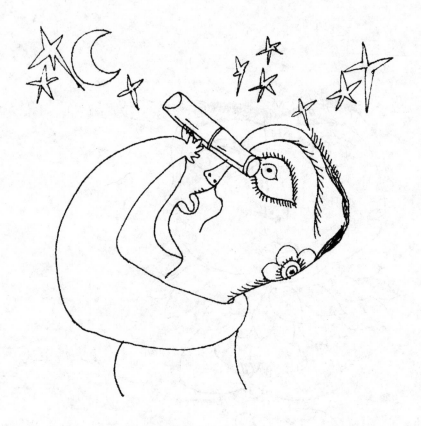

直 zhí   In ancient script, this character depicts a line of sight, and thus its original meaning was "straight". Also, because an honest person can squarely face up to others, it is used in the word for "正直（zhèngzhí：upright）". The famous modern writer Lu Xun, in his piece *Remembering Ms. Liu Hezhen*, wrote："真的猛士，敢于直面惨淡的人生，敢于正视淋漓的鲜血……（A true hero dares to opposite the gloomy life, dares to face the fresh, dripping blood…）" Using both "直面（zhímiàn）" and "正视（zhèngshì）" together in the description of a true hero, he brings out the literal meaning of "直".

xǐng

省 This character depicts a wide open, unmoving eye, thus meaning "to inspect" or "to observe". Today, we still say that to inspect or think over one's own behavior is "反省(fǎnxǐng：introspection)".

jiàn

见 The ancient form of this character protrudes an eye on the head of a person, indicating "看见(kànjiàn:to see)".

In ancient times, to see and to be seen were both written as "见". Later, to distinguish the two, to be seen by someone was written as "现(xiàn)", meaning "to make visible", "to show", or "to appear". A folk song, *Chile Valley* from the Northern and Southern Dynasties says: "风吹草低见牛羊。(Wind bending grass makes sheep and cattle visible.)" Here, "见" carries the meaning of "现(appear)".

The traditional form of "见" is written as "見".

60

mín
民 Ancient slave masters would deal with recalcitrant slaves by using the brutal punishment of piercing the eye. These disobedient slaves made up the largest group of people in the society of that day. Thus, "民" is a depiction of a horizontal eye being pierced, indicating disobedience. This sort of disobedient or surly facial expression is called by Beijingers "横 (pronounced hèng in the fourth tone)".

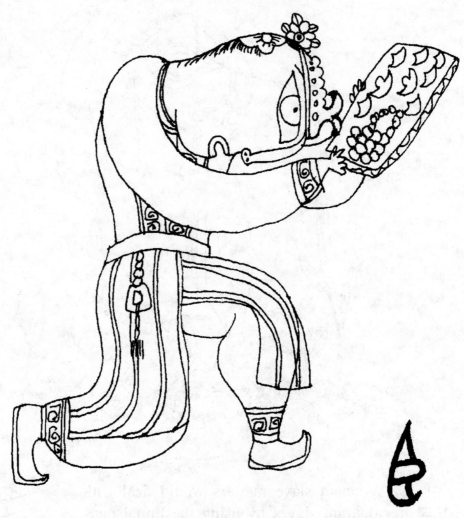

chén

臣   This character is the opposite of "民", referring to those obedient slaves in ancient times who were entrusted by their masters with higher duties, such as managing the "民" or slaves. These compliant slaves always downcast their eyes, not daring to look squarely at their masters. Thus, the traditional form of "臣" depicts an eye set on end, indicating one who is weak of will.

wàng

望   Ancient script used "臣" to mean "look", and the component "壬" expressed standing on the ground. Thus, the combination of "臣" and "壬" means to stand on the ground, gazing into the distance.

In the traditional form of the character, a "月" was added to make "朢". This character has been simplified to "望".

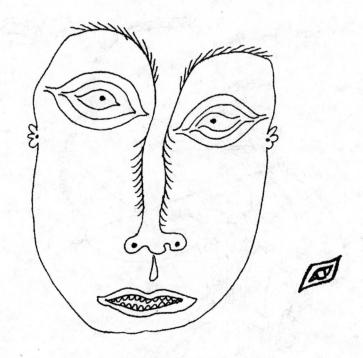

miàn   The ancient form of this character was in the shape of a face.
面   Because, of all the sense organs, the eye is the most prominent, the eye was drawn exaggerated.

Because the face is the most important feature of a human body, and the eye in turn is the most important feature of the face, the word "面目 (miànmù)" is often used to mean the appearance of people or situations. For example, a drastic change in appearance is called "面目全非(miàn mù quán fēi)", and something taking on a totally new look is called "面目一新(miàn mù yī xīn)".

There is a line of ancient Chinese poetry which reads: "不识庐山真面目,只缘身在此山中。(I can't tell what Mt. Lushan really looks like because I myself am in the mountain.)" "庐山真面目(lú shān zhēn miàn mù)" is often used as a metaphor for "the truth of a matter".

64

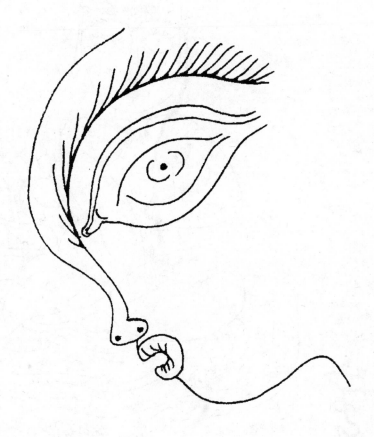

méi　　　This character originally depicted protruding hairs over an en-
眉　larged eye, thus it means "eyebrow".

　　　　Ancient people considered the eyes and eyebrows very important, and therefore they were extended to refer to looks or appearances in
general, as in the idiom "眉清目秀（méi qīng mù xiù）" or to the main
threads of a complicated affair, such as the word "眉目（méimù）".

mèi

媚

Ancient people thought that a woman's beauty was expressed mainly through the eyes, so in ancient writing "媚" was originally written as an enlarged eye and eyebrow on top of the figure of a woman, expressing the bright eyes and charm of a beautiful woman.

The Tang Dynasty poet Bai Juyi, in his *Song of Everlasting Regret*, wrote: "回眸一笑百媚生,六宫粉黛无颜色。(A glance with smile presents all her charm, all the beauties in imperial palace lose their radiance of attractiveness.)" His use of the character "媚(charm)" perfectly expresses the amorous glances coming from the eyes of the famous concubine, Yang Guifei.

ěr The ancient form of this charac-
耳 ter depicts an ear.

To strike someone about the
ears with one's palm is termed "打耳光(dǎ
ěrguāng)".

Things that are shaped like or resemble
ears also incorporate this character, such
as "木耳(mù'ěr: edible fungus)" and "银耳
(yín'ěr: tremella)".

wén

闻

In ancient script, this character depicts a man kneeling and holding a hand up to his ear, signifying "to listen".

The great Tang poet Meng Haoran once wrote in a poem: "春眠不觉晓,处处闻啼鸟。(This morning of spring in bed I'm lying, not awake till listening to birds' cry here and there.)" In this verse, "闻" means "to listen". Later, "闻" shifted to signify the function of the nose, rather than the function of the ear. Yet in such words as "耳闻 (ěrwén)" and "新闻(xīnwén)", "闻" still retains its original meaning.

The character has been standardized as "闻", with the "耳" component signifying the meaning, and the "门(mén)" component approximating its pronunciation.

^{zì}

自

This character originally depicted a nose. Because when referring to oneself, one often points to one's nose, this character came to mean "自己 (zìjǐ: self)". Hence, another character, "鼻 (bí)", was invented to mean "nose", with the "畀" component acting as a pronunciation clue, "bì".

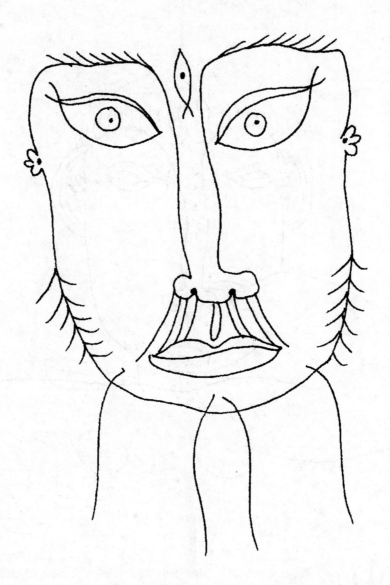

ér   The ancient form of this character is of facial hair—the form of long whiskers. In the character, the upper line represents the roots of the whiskers. The bottom portion is separated into two layers: the cheek whiskers and the chin whiskers. Later, "而" was adopted as a conjunction, and several other characters, "须(xū)" (traditional form: "鬚"), "鬍(hú)", and "髯(rán)" were created to mean "whiskers".

xū

须 "须" was created only after "而", originally meaning "whiskers", was borrowed as a conjunction.

This character depicts whiskers protruding from a person's face (represented by "页"). The three whiskers depicted here express a great number. The traditional form of the character is written as "鬚" ("髟" indicates something to do with hair).

The most noticeable quality about a man's face is his thick eyebrows and facial hair. Thus the word "须眉(xūméi: whiskers and eyebrows)" means "man".

口

kǒu   In ancient script, this is a depiction of a person's open
口   mouth, which is the original meaning of this character. Later,
       it was borrowed to apply to the openings of containers, as in
"碗口儿(wǎnkǒur：mouth of a bowl)" and "瓶口儿(píngkǒur：mouth
of a bottle）". It can also mean a passageway of some sort, as in "出
口儿 (chūkǒur: exit)" or "入口儿 (rùkǒur: entrance)". In these examples, it is pronounced "kǒur".

gān
甘

The ancient form of this character depicts a "口 (kǒu : mouth)" with a dash in the center to indicate a piece of food. Food that stays in the mouth must be sweet and delicious, which is the meaning of "甘美 (gānměi)" and "甘甜(gāntián)".

Because we love to eat good foods, "甘" has also taken on the meaning of "willing", as in "甘拜下风(gān bài xià fēng)", and "甘愿(gānyuàn)".

To be able to eat delicious foods is a kind of pleasure, and thus "甘" can also mean "happy" or "fortunate", as in "同甘共苦(tóng gān gòng kǔ)".

曰　　　　　yuē　　The form of the character is of a mouth with
　　　　　　　　　　a horizontal stroke, signifying breath and sound
曰　　　　　　　　　from the mouth and meaning to speak from the
mouth.

In ancient times when "说(shuō：say)" was not created, "曰" and "云" as in "子曰诗云(zǐ yuē shī yún)" were used to acquire the same meaning. "子" referred to Confucius and "子曰" in fact referred to *The Analects of Confucius* recording what was said by Confucius; "诗" referred to *The Book of Songs*, one of the classics venerated by Confucianists. Later generations have often used "子曰诗云" in referring to Confucianist classics.

"曰 (say)" and "日 (rì：day)" are written in the same way, but "曰" looks fat while "日" appears thin.

gǔ In the ancient form of this character, "口" indicates talking or narrating, and "十" refers to the age of creation of the heaven and earth. Therefore, the original meaning of "古" was to tell about the beginning of history. Because those events all took place in the distant past, we have the word "古代 (gǔdài)", meaning "ancient times".

chuī

吹

In ancient script, the character "欠" depicts a person with a wide-open mouth. By adding another "口 (kǒu: mouth)" on the left side to emphasize that breath comes out by way of the mouth, "吹" was created, meaning "to blow".

sī

司 This character originally depicted a person and a mouth, thus meaning one who issues orders.

From this meaning, it also carries the meanings of "to take charge", "to administer", or "to operate". For example, the operator of a train, car, or other vehicle is called "司机(sījī)". The actions of law enforcement agencies that investigate and judge civil and criminal cases are known as "司法(sīfǎ)".

lìng
令
In the ancient form of this character, the top portion resembles a mouth, giving orders, while the bottom part is a kneeling person, obedient to commands. Thus, "令" means "下令 (xiàlìng: to issue orders)", or "命令 (mìnglìng: to order, orders)".

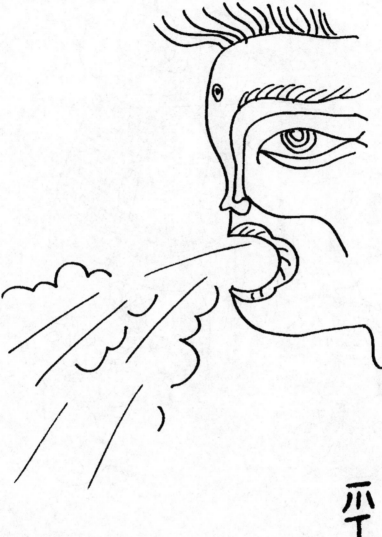

乎

hū   In ancient script the character resembles waves coming from sound, meaning "呼叫(hūjiào: to call)". Ancient people often used "乎" as an interjection as in "之乎者也(zhī hū zhě yě)". Later a "口" was added to carry the original meaning.

xiāo

嚻 This character is composed of "页 (meaning 'head')" and four mouths. A lot of people talking together results in a confusing chatter, so this character means an uproar, bustle, or hubbub, as in "叫嚻 (jiàoxiāo)" and "喧嚻(xuānxiāo)".

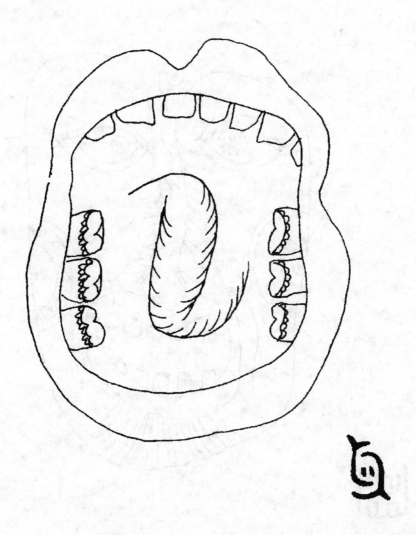

yá

牙 The ancient form of this character shows an open mouth, with both sides displaying molars, which are colloquially called "槽牙(cáoyá)" or "大牙(dàyá)".

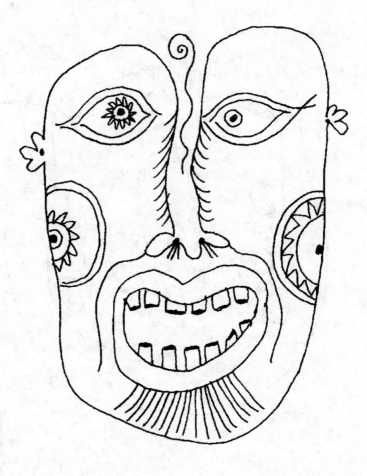

chǐ

齿 In ancient script, this character is a depiction of alternating upper and lower teeth. Later, a "止(zhǐ)" was added to approximate the pronunciation.

The traditional form of this character is written as "齒".

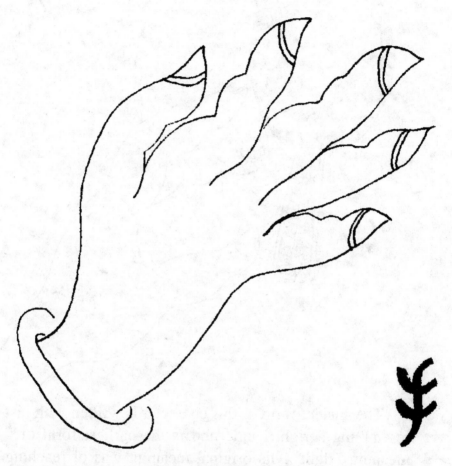

shǒu

手   The ancient form of this character was of a hand with five fingers. As a component of another character, it often appears as "扌" which is named "提手 (tíshǒu：carrying hand)" or written as "手(hand)".

Hands are used to engage in work. Thus, when someone has mastered a particular skill or is an expert in certain aspect, they are often described as a "手", as in "选手 (xuǎnshǒu：candidate)", "能手(néngshǒu：ace)", or "多面 手(duōmiànshǒu：a many-sided person, a generalist)".

yòu   The ancient form of this character is written with just three lines,
又 resembling a right hand, and is the earliest form of "右(yòu)",
meaning "right". Its original meaning was of reaching out to give
assistance. In ancient characters, the number three is often used to indicate
a large number; here it represents the five fingers of a hand. Later, the
character was standardized to simply "又".

Later, "又" was written as "右" and used to indicate a direction: right
while "右" meaning to help was written as "佑(yòu)". In ancient times,
"右" carrying the meaning of respect meant a higher position. For example, it is recorded in *Records of Historian*, *Lian Po and Lin Xiangru Biographies* that Lin Xiangru was appointed *Shangqing* for his outstanding
contribution, positioned Lian Po to the right.

Later, "又" became an adverb indicating repetition.

jí 　　This character depicts a right hand grasp-
及　ing a person, meaning "赶上（gǎnshàng：to
　　catch）", "逮住（dǎizhù：to capture）".

Today when we say "及格（jígé）", it means to
reach a qualifying level, reflecting the original
meaning of "及".

yǒu

友

This character originally depicted two right hands, meaning two people helping each other. In ancient times, the word "友于(yǒuyú)" referred to the feelings between brothers, because such a relationship expresses solidarity and fraternal love.

Two hands clasping indicates friendly feelings between two people, so "友" is now found in the word for "朋友(péng·you: friends)".

86

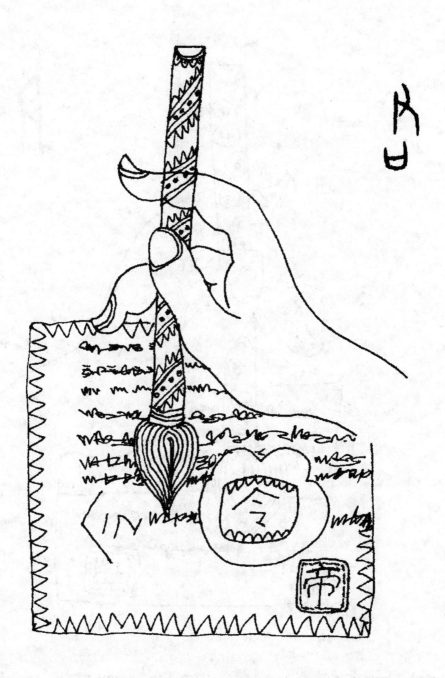

jūn   In ancient script, this character is a representation
君 of a right hand holding a writing brush, with a "口
(kǒu: mouth)" added to signify the giving of orders.
Thus, it means "君" as in "君主(jūnzhǔ: sovereign)".

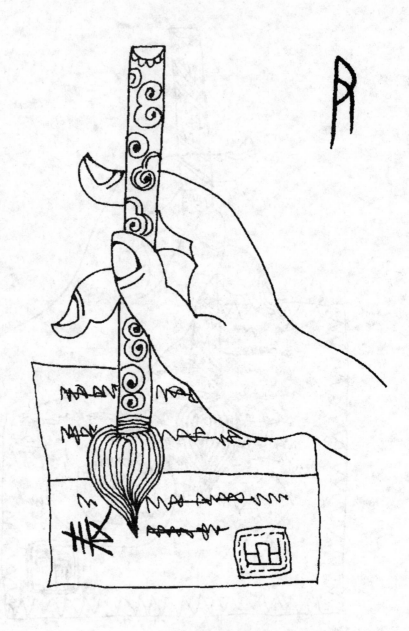

yǐn　　　This character shows a right hand holding a

尹　pen, which is represented by the vertical stroke.

　　　"尹" in ancient times was an official title, and
is now often used as a surname.

fù

父

The ancient form of this character is the shape of a hand-held stone axe, and actually means "斧(fǔ:axe)".

In ancient times, most stone-workers were men, and thus "斧" later came to mean "父" as in "父亲(fù·qīn: father)".

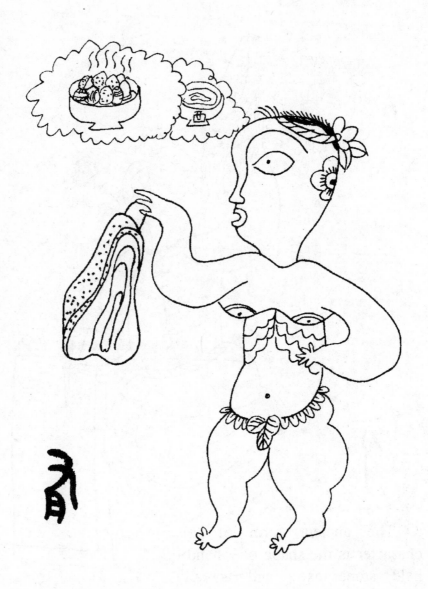

yǒu   The character originally depicted a right hand holding
有   a piece of meat. To have something in hand gave birth to
the meaning "拥有(yōngyǒu: to possess)", later came to
mean "有(to have)".

qī

妻   The ancient form of this character is of hands grabbing the long hair of a woman, and means "妻子 (qī · zi: wife)". The ancient form of this character reflects the practice of ancient society of forcefully seizing a woman to be one's mate.

qǔ   This character originally showed a right hand
取   clutching an ear.

Ancient warriors would cut off the left ears of captured enemies to make a tally of a military victory, which was
the original meaning of "取". Because an enemy prisoner's ear
must be cut off by a soldier himself, "取" also has the meaning
of obtaining or taking something for oneself, which is how it is
used today.

qǔ 娶 To make, take or receive a young woman as one's wife is "娶 (to marry)". "女" indicates that the object of action of "娶" is a woman, and "取" both expresses the action of "娶 (to marry, take as one's wife)" and the pronunciation.

婢
bì

In ancient script, this character is the image of a woman holding a large fan, depicting the imperial maids who would fan the emperor from behind with a large fan. These serving girls in ancient times were always in close proximity to the sovereign or the aristocracy, so later we called all personal maids "婢".

zhuǎ

爪

This character is in the shape of a hand reaching out to grasp or clutch something, and thus only shows three fingers. The character, when used as a component of other characters, is often crowned thereto and written as " ⺥ ".

Ancient people, when creating characters, often used the number three to indicate a lot of something; here, the three lines represent the five fingers of a hand.

fú 孚 The ancient form of this character shows a hand clutching a person, meaning "俘虏（fúlǔ: prisoner of war）", or "俘获（fúhuò: to capture）". Later, a "亻" was added to make "俘".

"孚" later came to mean "to inspire confidence", as in the phrase "深孚众望（shēn fú zhòng wàng: to enjoy great popularity）".

yìn

印 This character depicts a hand pushing down on someone, forcing him to kneel. Thus, the original meaning of "印" was "按(àn: push down)", "压(yā: press down)".

Because when using a chop or a seal, one must also press down, "印" later came to mean "印章(yìnzhāng: chop)".

fú　　Ancient script depicts this character as a hand pressing
服　down on a kneeling person, and means "制服 (zhìfú: to
　　place under control)", "降服（xiángfú：to subdue)".
　　The original form was "𝙖" and later a "月（肉月 'flesh'）"
was added to form "服".

妥 tuǒ The ancient form of this character depicts a hand firmly pressing down on a woman, making her sit upright, thus meaning "安定（āndìng: stable）". Later, "妥" came to mean "妥当（tuǒ·dang: proper, appropriate）".

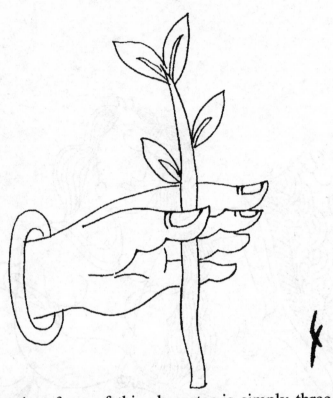

zuǒ   The ancient form of this character is simply three lines to represent a left hand. The left hand cooperates with the right hand to

左 do things, so it originally meant "佐助(zuǒzhù:to help)". Later, "左" was used to mean "left", and the character "佐" was created to express the original meaning "辅佐(fǔzuǒ:to assist)".

In ancient times, "左" also carried the meaning of respect in relation to riding in a coach or a horse and therefore, people often said "虚左以待 (xū zuǒ yǐ dài: to wait for someone with the left seat vacant)". With this exception, pre-Qin people gave precedence to the right over the left and so a reduced position was called "左迁(zuǒqiān:a shift to the left)". In ancient times, a palace had three gates and the one in the middle was called "正门(zhèngmén:main entrance, '正' also metaphorically means just and honorable)". Therefore, "左" also carries the meaning of "不正 (bùzhèng: dishonest)" as in "旁门左道(páng mén zuǒ dào: heterodox school)" as well as in "左嗓子(zuǒsǎng·zi:singing out of key)". Ancient contracts were made in both left and right parts, the left part going to the creditor as proof, so the record was also termed "左证(zuǒzhèng: evidenced by left part)".

cùn　　The ancient form of this character depicts an indicating dot under a hand, showing a spot about one inch from the palm, where the veins are. The traditional Chinese medical term "寸口 (cùnkǒu: entrance of pulse)" embodies the intentions of creating the character. Later, it was incorporated into "尺寸 (chǐcùn)", measurement of length or size.

zhēng   This character originally depicted
争   two hands struggling over an object,
     from which the meaning "to contend,
to strive" is derived.

gǒng

拱 This character, in ancient script, depicts two hands clasped together, which is a form of respectful greeting.

Today this character is written as "拱". As a component of another character, it appears as "廾" or "大", as in "弄（nòng：to do, to fool with）" and "樊（fán：fence, or a surname）".

chéng

丞

The ancient form of this character depicts two hands trying to rescue a person who has fallen into a trap, and is a component of "拯" as in "拯救 (zhěngjiù: to save, to rescue)".

From this meaning of saving one who has come into dire circumstances, "丞" means "to help". For example, one who assisted the sovereign in managing state affairs was called "丞相(chéngxiàng: the prime minister)", here pronounced "chéng", while the original meaning of the character is now expressed by adding a " 扌 " to make "拯", pronounced "zhěng".

104

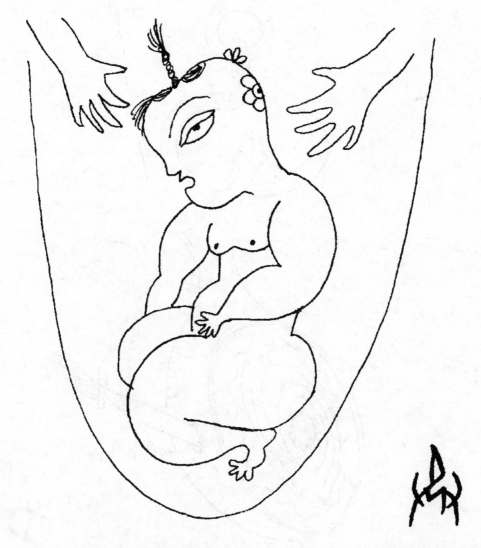

chéng

承

The original form of this character depicted two hands holding up another person.

From the point of view of the person being held, this signifies "接受 (jiēshòu)", "承受 (chéngshòu)", "承接 (chéngjiē)" or "to carry on", "to endure". Today, the character "承" as in "继承 (jìchéng: to inherit, carry on)" still uses this meaning. From the original form of two hands holding up another, we derive the phrase "奉承 (fèng·cheng: to flatter)".

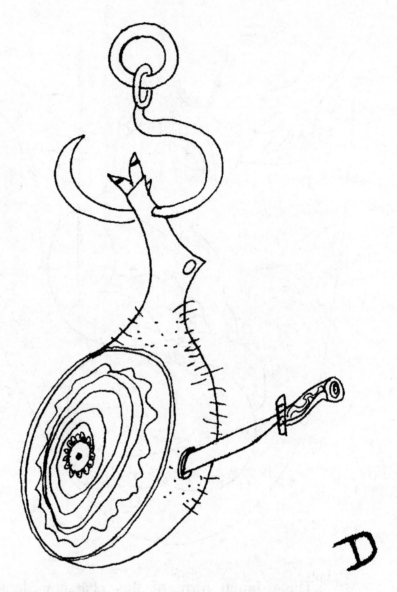

ròu

肉   In ancient script, this character is a depiction of a large chunk of meat. When it appears as a component of another character, it signifies a part or organ of a person (or animal), and is written as "月" or "月" which is commonly called "肉月旁 (ròuyuèpáng: a side component formed of a chunk of meat in the shape of a crescent moon)".

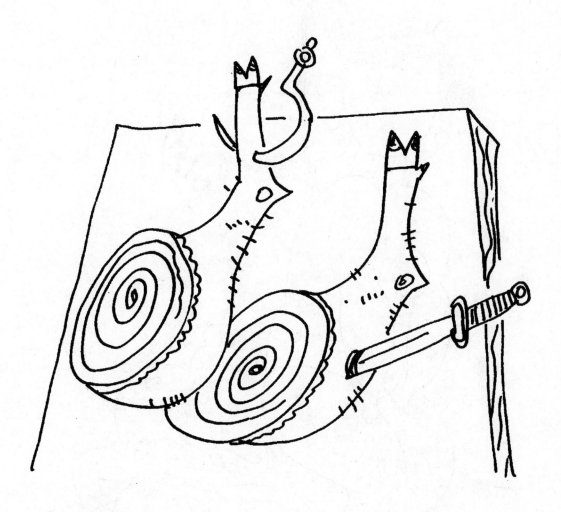

duō 多 The ancient form of the character is a depiction of two pieces of meat, indicating a great number or a lot, and later evolved into a combination of two "夕 (evening)" written as "多", but the meaning is not related to "夕" as in "夕阳(xīyáng：a setting sun)".

yù

育　　This character was originally formed by a "女 (nǚ: a woman)" and an upside-down "子 (zǐ: a child)", thus depicting a mother giving birth to a child. It means "养育 (yǎngyù: to raise, to rear)".

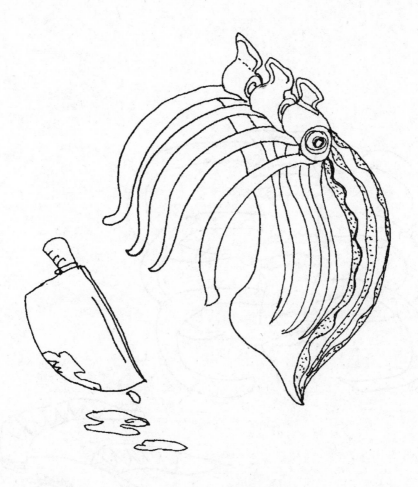

gǔ

骨

The upper half of this character represents a cut-through bone, while the bottom half is meat, thus signifying a bone with meat still on it.

The construction of "骨" illustrates that "骨" and "肉" are interdependent and inseparable. We often use the phrase "骨肉 (gǔròu)" to refer to blood connections among the parents, siblings, children, as in "骨肉团聚 (gǔ ròu tuán jù: reunion of the family members)" and "亲生骨肉(qīn shēng gǔ ròu: child borne by oneself)".

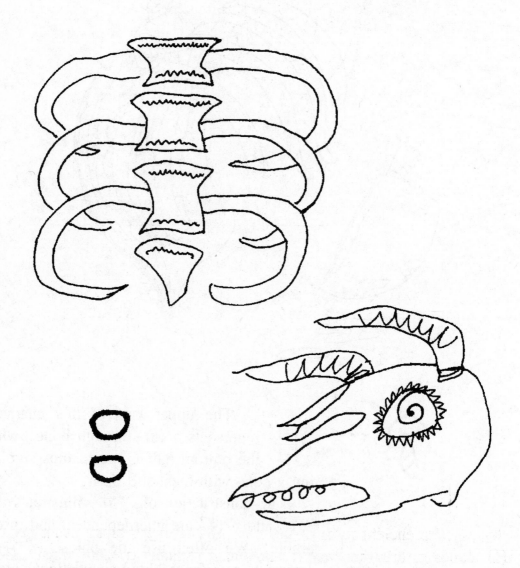

lǚ The ancient form of this character represents the 吕 backbone of a person or an animal. Today it is mostly used as a surname or the name of a place.

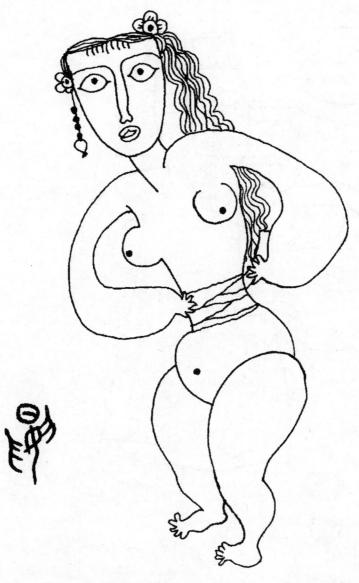

yāo   The ancient form of this character is of a woman using her two
要   hands to bind her waist, and thus originally meant "waist". This
     was the initial form of "腰(yāo:waist)" and later a "月(a piece of
meat in the shape of a crescent moon)" was added thereto to signify this
meaning. Then "要" is mostly used to mean "要求(yāoqiú:to demand)".

The original form of "要" shows that the practice of women restricting
their waists to appear beautiful was prevalent even in ancient times.

shèng   The ancient form of this character shows a person
圣 (represented by "王" signifying an upright posture) with an
ear close to a mouth, meaning expansive knowledge and
tireless teaching.

The first great teacher in China's history was Confucius, who is
respectfully known as "孔圣人(kǒngshèngrén:the Sage)".

The traditional form of this character is written as"聖".

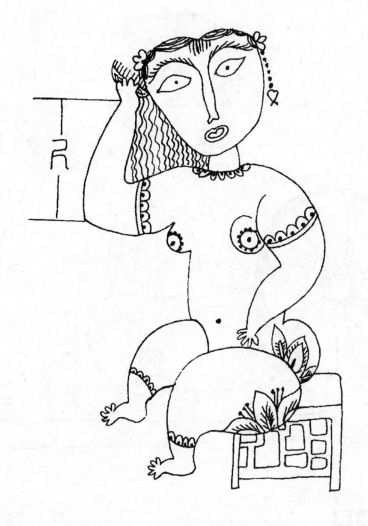

chǐ

尺

Ancient people used the length of a man's forearm as a standard unit of measuring length, which is about the length of a "尺(Chinese foot, being about an English foot)" that came into use at a later time. In other languages, such as English and Arabic, different limbs were also used to represent various units of length.

咫

zhǐ 　　 Another ancient unit of measurement, "咫" is derived from
咫 the length of a woman's arm. Because a woman's arm is shorter
　　 than a man's, a "咫" is thus shorter than a "尺", and is about
8/10 of a Chinese foot.

　　"咫尺" symbolizes a very short distance as in the idiom "咫尺天涯
(zhǐ chǐ tiān yá：so near and yet so far)".

xún　　This character originally was an ancient unit for measuring length, equal to the span of a person's outstretched arms.

寻

A person with outstretched arms seems to be expecting something, and so "寻" also means "to look for", as in "追寻(zhuīxún：to pursue)" and "寻求(xúnqiú：to seek, explore)".

yù   The ancient form of this character is composed of teeth, a 与 mouth, and several interlocking hands, indicating a group of people discussing or planning something, and meaning "参与 (cānyù: to participate)". On modern diplomatic occasions, the words "与国(yùguó)" and "与会者(yùhuìzhě)", meaning "countries attending a conference" and "participant", are often used.

The traditional form of this character is written as "與".

guǐ

鬼

During ancient ancestor worship rites, a person would wear a mask and dress up as a deceased ancestor. Thus, "鬼" in ancient script represents a deceased ancestor.

In the Han Dynasty, a person's spirit after death was called "鬼".

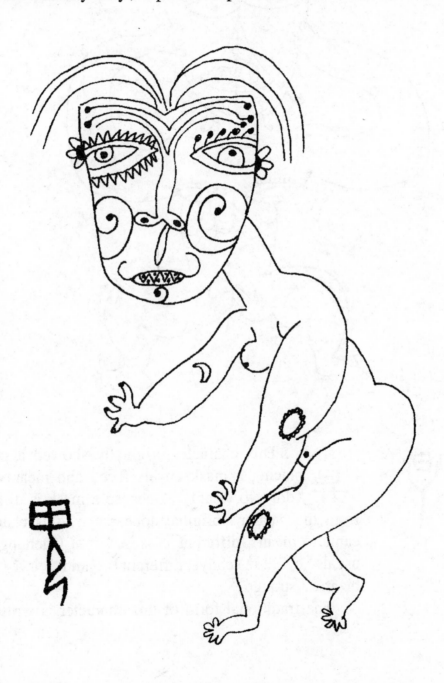

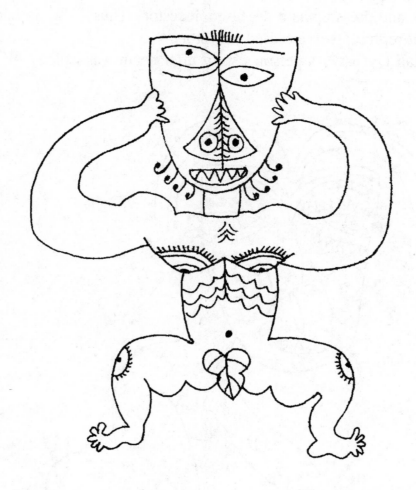

yì

异

This character originally showed a person placing a mask on his face, and meant "戴 (dài: to wear)". Because a mask is different from the wearer's original appearance, this character came to mean "different", as in "异常 (yìcháng: unusual)", "差异 (chāyì: different)", and "奇异 (qíyì: bizarre, strange)".

The traditional form of this character is written as "異".

zhǐ

止

The ancient form of this character is of the left and right feet. Later, the left foot was written as "止" and the right foot as " ⺀ (dá)". When "止 (zhǐ)" came to be used in "停止 (tíngzhǐ:to stop)", a new character,"趾(zhǐ)" was adopted to indicate a person's toes. The component "足 (zú)" indicates the lower limbs while "止" expresses the meaning and gives the pronunciation.

xiān

先 The top portion of this character is a "止" and the lower portion a "儿(indicating 人: man)". In ancient script, "止" being placed before a "人(rén: man)" means to precede and is standardized "先". In ancient writings "先" often referred to a deceased person. For example, Zhuge Liang wrote in his *Memorial on Dispatching Troops* submitted to Liu Chan, the Monarch of the Kingdom of Shu Han: "先帝不以臣卑鄙……(The former Monarch did not treat me as a mere subject …)" Here "先帝(xiāndì: the former Monarch)" referred to deceased Liu Bei.

"先生(xiān·sheng)" was used by ancient people to refer to people who were older and more learned than oneself, and later to men, especially older men. Now it is used to refer to both men and women, who are learned or respected.

120

此

In ancient script, "匕 (bì)" is a "人 (rén: man)" written in reversed writing order, and "止 (zhǐ)" refers to the toes. The character was formed by "匕" and "止", signifying the position of a person's toes, and therefore, some scholars held the meaning to be "this position". *The Book of Songs, Section Xiao Ya, Shao Zhi Hua* says: "知我如此，不如无生。(Should it be known I am like this, rather than I were not borne.)" Here "此" means "这样 (zhèyàng: like this)".

In modern language, "此" as a pronoun is often used against "彼 (bǐ)", for example, "彼此 (each other)" and "此一时，彼一时 (That was one situation and this is another)".

之 zhī In ancient script, the top portion of this character is a "止(zhǐ: left foot, people when walking usually make a first step with the left foot)", indicating walking. The horizontal line in the bottom portion represents the place where one is heading. Thus the original meaning of "之" was "往 (wǎng: towards)". The phrase from the Chinese classic *Mencius* "先生将何之" means "Where are you going, sir?"

Later, "之" came to be used as a pronoun for a person or an object or an auxiliary word similar to "的(·de)".

 zú
足

The ancient form of this character resembles "legs and feet". Hence the meaning.

"足" as a component, often appears on the left or the bottom of another character, indicating the position, movements of legs and feet and other objects having to do with "脚 (jiǎo: feet)", as in "趾 (zhǐ: toes)", "跑 (pǎo: to run)", "蹩 (bié: sprained foot)" as well as in "路 (lù: road)".

"足" appearing on the left of another character is written as "𧾷".

bù

步 One foot in front of the other represents one step, so the ancient script put a "止 (zhǐ: left foot)" and a "少 (dá: right foot)" together to form "步 (step)". "止" occupies the top portion because usually the left foot makes the first step.

124

qǐ

企

Ancient script depicts the exaggerated toes of a person, as if he is standing on tiptoe. This is a pose of craving something earnestly, so hoping to obtain some object or goal is known as "企求(qǐqiú)" or "企望(qǐwàng)". Penguins, which walk upright, are called "企鹅(qǐé)".

 zǒu

走 The top portion of this character originally depicted a person running, with arms swinging out, taking large strides. The bottom half consists of a "止 (zhǐ)", emphasizing the action of running. Thus, originally, "走" meant "奔跑 (bēnpǎo: to run)".

"走" in the idiom "走马观花 (zǒu mǎ guān huā: to look at flowers while riding a horse)" still adheres to the original meaning.

Later, "走" came to mean "步行 (bùxíng: to walk)".

wěi

尾   The ancient form of this character resembles a person with a large tail. This was actually a form of dress for ancient slaves, and meant "lowly, humble". Later it came to be extended to indicate the latter portion of something, as in "首尾相接（shǒu wěi xiāng jiē：to make the head and tail or beginning and end connected)" and "尾随（wěisuí：to follow at one's heels)".

    "尾" also came to be used to indicate the tail of an animal, as in the word "尾巴（wěi·ba)".

dǎi   This character depicts a hand clutching a tail,
逮   meaning "逮住 (dǎizhù: to capture)". The original
form of the character is "隶 (pronounced dǎi)", but
because capturing something is always accompanied by
walking, the component "辶" is added to make "逮".

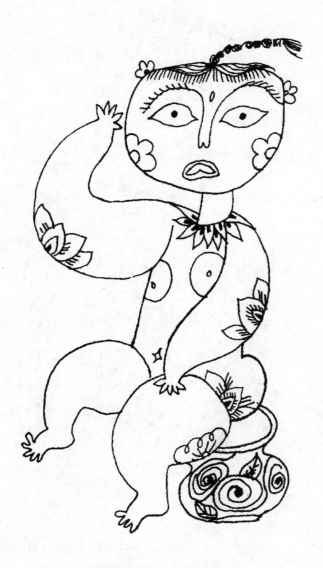

shǐ

屎 Ancient script depicts this character as several dots under the figure of a person, meaning "faeces".

 wú   The ancient form of this character
无   shows a person carrying a hairy ornament
      or decoration (such as an ox tail) in each
hand, meaning "dance". Its traditional form is
written as "無".

Later, "無" was used to mean "not have",
and a "舛 (chuǎn, indicating two feet back to
back)" was added underneath it to mean dancing.

xià In ancient script, this character represents a complete person, and carries the meaning of a perfect person.

夏 The area in modern-day Shaanxi and Shanxi provinces was one of the birthplaces of Chinese culture. People there used the word（夏）to mean "large" or "grand". People all over the world respect and honor themselves, and today we have the word "华夏（huáxià）" representing our country as in ancient time, meaning "prosperous, perfect, and great".

SECTION TWO

NATURE

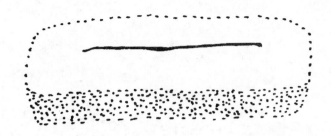

yī   In ancient script, the horizontal stroke "一(one)" represents
the beginning of positive round figures.

Xu Shen said at the beginning of *Narration and Explanation
of Characters*: "惟初太极，道立于一；造分天地，化成万物。(Ever since
the beginning of the universe, doctrines have been based on '一[one]';
It created and separated the heaven and earth and gave birth to everything.)" Here "一(one)" represented the heavenly doctrine dominating
the heaven and earth, or in other words, the human world separated from
"一(one)", the heavenly doctrine. This is the thought of Xu Shen's phi-
losophy and explains why he put "一(one)" at the beginning of the opening chapter.

In modern Chinese, many word groups are formed with "一(one)"
but with differing pronunciations. An individual "一(one)" or when it
follows another character is pronounced "yī" in the first tone as in "统一
(tǒngyī: unification)", "万一(wànyī: in case)"; it is pronounced in the
fourth tone when characters following it are pronounced in the first, second or third tone as in "一边(yībiān: on one side)", "一直(yīzhí: straight
on)", "一起(yīqǐ: altogether)"; it is pronounced in the second tone when
characters following it are pronounced in the fourth tone as in "一个(yī·
ge: one piece)", "一定(yīdìng: surely, must)", "一共(yīgòng: altogether, in all)".

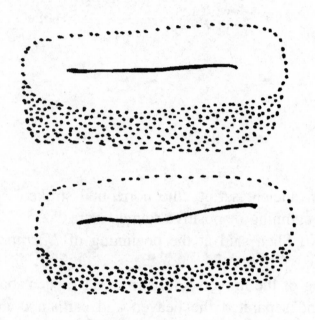

èr　　In ancient script, two horizontal strokes with differing length
⎯　indicates "二(two)".

⎯　　It is said in *The Book of Changes* that "天一地二,有一然后有
二。(The heaven is represented by '一[one]' while the earth by '二
[two]', '一[one]' preceding '二[two]'.)" Therefore, "二(two)" also refers to the earth. When a component was added between the two
horizontal strokes, the upper stroke referred to the heaven and the bottom one referred to the earth as in "亘(gèn)".

136

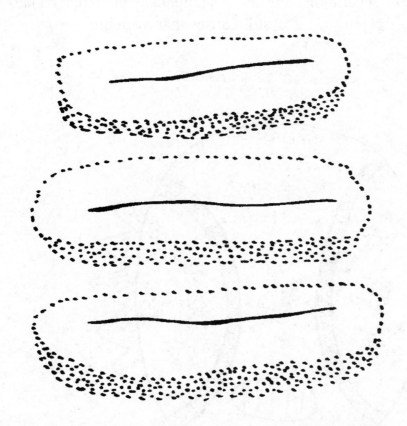

sān   In ancient script, "三(three)" represents the number three.

The first of the eight trigrams, the heaven trigram, as represented by "三", the three horizontal strokes respectively representing the heaven, the earth and the people, or in other words, it included everything in heaven, on earth and in the human world. For this reason, Lao Zi said: "One gives birth to two, two gives birth to three and three gives birth to everything." This explains why in ancient script "三(three)" often referred to a lot or a great many, as in "三令五申(sān lìng wǔ shēn: order repeatedly given)", "三思而行(sān sī ér xíng: to consider again and again before you act)".

bā

八

In ancient script, two bent lines back to back carries the meaning of separation. When it came to be used to indicate the number eight, an individual "八 (eight)" no longer meant separation, but as a component of another character as in "分 (fēn)", "八" still carries that meaning.

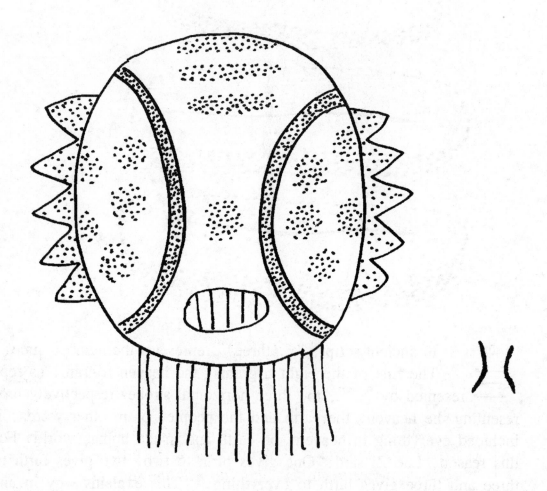

rì 日   This character is a representation of the sun. When appearing as a component of another character, it indicates something to do with the sun, as in "光明（guāngmíng：bright）", "照耀（zhàoyào：to illuminate）", and "温暖（wēnnuǎn：warm）".

dàn

In ancient script, this character depicts a sun which has just risen over the horizon, indicating the break of dawn. A line of shadow underneath shows that the sun has not totally left the horizon.

zǎo

早

"十" in ancient script means "to split, to rupture". By adding a sun on top, this character indicates the moment when the sun breaks through the darkness of night—dawn, as in "早晨 (zǎo·chen: early in the morning)".

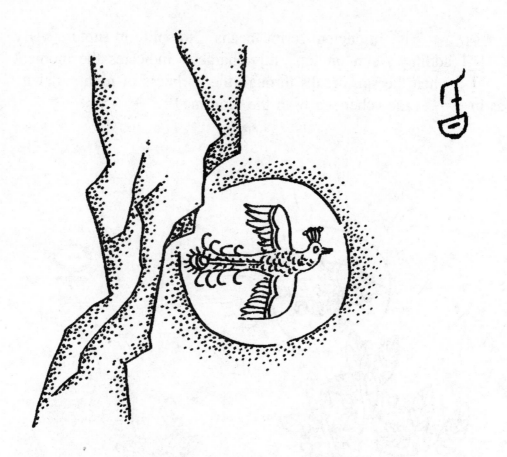

hūn

昏　　In ancient script, "氐" is also written as "氐", meaning underneath. "氐" coming on top of "日", resembling a falling sun, means "黄昏（huánghūn：dusk）" which refers to the time just before it gets quite dark. Then, the character also carries the meaning of "昏暗（hūn'àn：dim）". For example, Du Fu wrote in his poem *Autumn Wind Piercing Thatched Cottage*："俄顷风定云墨色,秋天漠漠向昏黑。(The clouds are turning dark just after wind died down, Dusk is falling in the vast loneliness of an Autumn day.)"

In ancient times, as wedding ceremonies were held at dusk, the character also took on the meaning of "结婚（jiēhūn：marriage）" as it is said in *The Book of Songs, Song of Bei State, Gu Feng*："燕尔新昏,如兄如弟。(Attendants entertained at your wedding are like brothers.)" To distinguish from "昏" in "黄昏（dusk）", "女（nǚ：woman）" was added to make "婚（marriage）".

shì
是   The morning sun gives people light. In ancient script the addition of "止" below "旱（zǎo：morning）" indicates the pursuit of light, implying "correct". The character was later standardized as "是".

The idioms "实事求是（shí shì qiú shì：to seek truth from facts）" and "自以为是（zì yǐ wéi shì：to consider oneself right）" preserve the original meaning of "是". Today, "是" is also used as a grammatical term to show relations between things.

yùn
晕　The ancient form of this character depicts halos of light from the sun (or the moon) shining through layers of clouds, respectively called "日晕(rìyùn：solar halo)" and "月晕(yuèyùn：lunar halo)".

Later, this character was written as "晕", with "日" representing the sun, and "军(jūn：army)" representing part of the meaning (as the clouds are like war chariots which encircle the sun, closing it in; see the separate entry for "军") and also approximating the pronunciation.

xī 昔 In distant ages past, disastrous floods were common, and were unforgettable for those who experienced them. The ancient form of "昔" is of a sun hanging over flowing waters, indicating days gone by are still fresh in memory. Thus, its original meaning was "往昔 (wǎngxī: former days)".

jīng

晶

In ancient script, this character represents a multitude of stars, and actually means "star".

Because stars shine bright, this character has come to mean "光亮(guāngliàng：luminous)" in modern Chinese.

146

xīng

星

In ancient script, this character is written as "晶（jīng）" with a "生（shēng）" below it, indicating those heavenly bodies which shine in the night. In the standard form of the character, "晶" has been simplified to "日（rì）", and "生" approximates the pronunciation.

yuè
月

A full moon appears on the evening of August 15 of the lunar calendar, which reminds people of "团圆 (tuányuán: family reunion)". On that evening, family members gather under the full moon, while enjoying happiness, longing for those of kin far away from them. The day is also termed Mid‑Autumn Festival, one of the significant traditional days.

To distinguish it from "日 (rì: the sun)", "月 (the moon)" in ancient script depicts the sliver of a new moon. The dot in the middle is not necessarily present until it is needed to distinguish it from "夕 (xī: evening, night)".

Su Dongpo of the Song Dynasty wrote: "人有悲欢离合, 月有阴晴圆缺, 此事古难全。(Either parted or reunited people may feel grieved or happy; Either waning or waxing the moon may appear shadowed or bright. Nothing of that kind can be perfect ever since the ancient times.)" "缺 (quē: wax)" refers to the sliver of the moon. Since ancient times, people do not know how much care and thought wane and wax of the moon have caused them to give to their kin.

"月 (the moon)" is also used as a component in other characters, indicating something to do with the moon or time.

The difference between "月" and "月 (肉月)" is that the first stroke of the former is written "丿" while that of the latter is written "丨".

148

xī

夕   The ancient form of this character represents a half moon, indicating evening, when the moon begins to shine.

Li Shangyin of the late Tang Dynasty wrote in his *Climb Le You Yuan*: "夕阳无限好，只是近黄昏。(So beautiful is the setting sun, Only dusk is coming.)" In opposite use of the meaning, Marshal Ye Jianying wrote in his *Lyric at Eighty*: "老夫喜作黄昏颂，满目青山夕照明。(Compared to dusk, I'd like to be an old man, Green mountains in view are bright in the setting sun.)" "夕" in this context means dusk.

To distinguish from "月 (yuè)", "夕" in ancient script has no stroke in the center. The character is standardized as "夕".

míng
名

"夕（xī）" represents a half moon, meaning dark night while "口（kǒu）" represents a person's mouth.

Because people could not be clearly seen in the moon light, the ancient form is a combination of "夕" and "口" and means to tell one's own name. From this meaning, it took on the meaning of "说出 (shuōchū：to say)", "说明（shuōmíng：to explain)", as in idioms "莫名 其妙（mò míng qí miào：cannot tell the reason)" and "不可名状（bù kě míng zhuàng：beyond description)".

In ancient times, "名（name）" and "字（zì：style）" differed. A noble man was given a name at birth and a style after a solemn hat-wearing ceremony at the age of twenty. Later, the name was used by the man himself while others called him by the style to show respect. The meanings of name and style were interrelated, for example, Li Bai, the poet-immortal, was named Bai and styled Tai Bai; and Du Fu, the poet-sage, was named Fu (Fu means the laudatory title for men) and styled Zi Mei (Mei means handsome, beautiful). In modern times, the practice of using a name and a style has been abandoned and people are now called only by name.

míng

明

The ancient form of this character resembles a moon shining through an open window. In the darkness of the night, the moon appears to be brighter than the sun, hence the use of "明" in "明亮 (míngliàng: bright)".

The great Tang poet Li Bai wrote in his poem "静夜思 (*Thoughts at a Silent Night*)": "床前明月光，疑是地上霜。举头望明月，低头思故乡。(Before bed, light is cast from the moon, It's frost I do suspect. With head raised, I stare at the bright moon, Lowering my head, I miss my native town.)" The use of "明" here embodies precisely the meaning its creators endowed it with.

This character had been written as "囧月", but the "囧", representing a window, was later changed to "日", resulting in the present-day "明".

sù

夙

In ancient script, this character depicts a person laboring under the moon, indicating someone who has risen early. This character thus means "early".

It is written in *The Book of Songs*: "夙兴夜寐，靡有朝矣，" depicting a scene of a woman working from dawn until dusk. Today, this character is often used in describing an indomitable working spirit.

yǔ

雨

This character depicts falling rain-drops, and thus of course, means "rain". When used as a component of another character, "雨" indicates something to do with the weather.

líng **零** In ancient script, this character depicts rain, indicating the act of raining. Later, it was written as "零", "雨 (yǔ)" referring to rain and "令 (lìng)" providing the pronunciation.

The earliest collection of Chinese poetry, *The Book of Songs* has a verse "零雨其濛 (líng yǔ qí méng)", expressing a misty, drizzly scene of nature. "零雨" means "to drizzle".

Because raindrops are small, "零" means "零碎 (língsuì: fragmentary or tiny, trivial)". For example, a weather report may say, "零星小雨 (líng xīng xiǎo yǔ)", meaning "occasional showers".

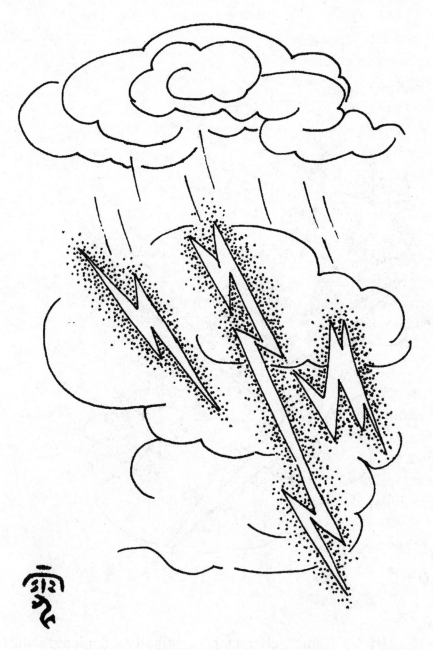

diàn

电

The ancient form of this character shows rain accompanied by lightening, and originally meant "lightening".

The traditional form of this character is written as "電", and is now standardized as "电".

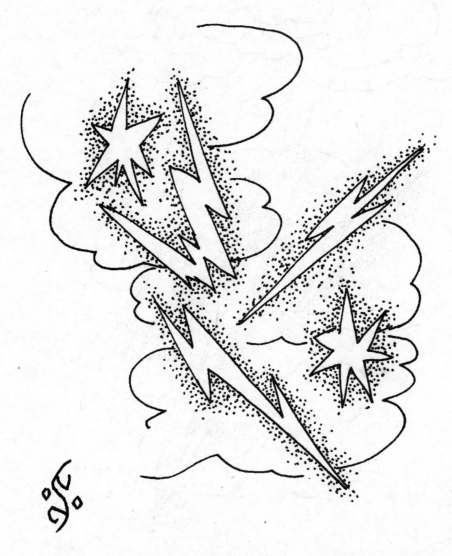

léi   This character originally depicted the
雷 sound of thunder and lightening, and meant
"thunder".

The traditional form of this character is written as
"靁" and is now standardized as "雷".

yún

云

The ancient form of this character depicts a layer of clouds with a wisp curling up beneath. Later, because clouds are often associated with rain, it was written as "雲"; the modern simplified character is written in its original form.

shēn 申 In ancient script, this character depicts a flash of lightning in the clouds, and means "lightning". Because the wave of lightning seems to be stretching out to something, this character by inference means " 屈伸 (qūshēn: to bend and stretch)" and by adding " 亻", " 伸 " is formed, further means "伸张 (shēnzhāng: to support, uphold)".

qì 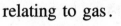 The ancient form of this character resembles wisps of steam or vapor curling over themselves. To distinguish it from "乞(qǐ)", a "米" is added to make "氣". The simplified version has returned to the original "气".

As a component of another character, "气" indicates something relating to gas.

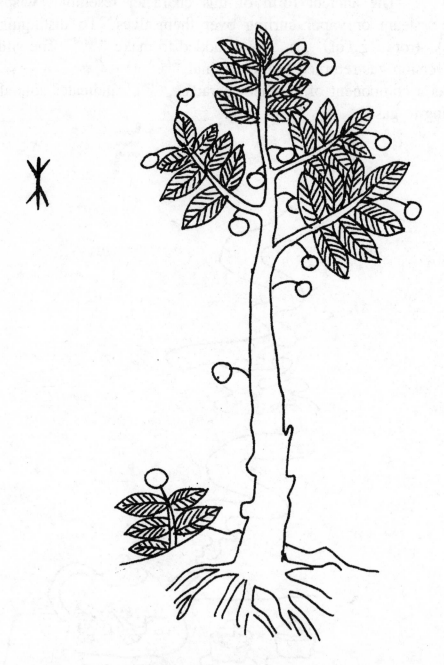

mù 木　　With the top half resembling branches and the bottom half resembling roots, this character resembles a "tree" in ancient script.

　　As a character component, "木" most often appears on the left or on the bottom, and indicates something to do with trees or wood.

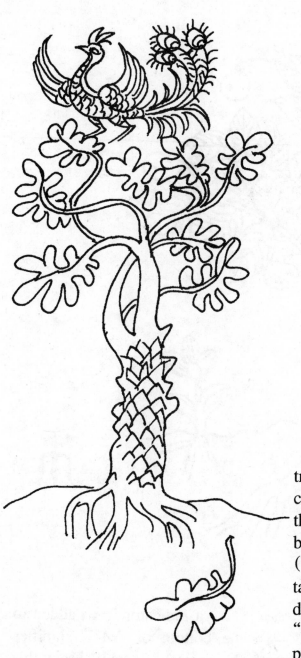

mò

末

An indicator "一" added to the top of "木" indicates the top of a tree, which is the meaning of this character in ancient script. From this, two other meanings have been derived: one is "不重要的 (bù zhòngyào · de: not important)" or "非根本的(fēi gēnběn · de: incidental)" as in the idiom "本末倒置(běn mò dào zhì: to put the incidental before the fundamental)"; the other is "最后 (zuìhòu: last)", as in "末了 (mòliǎo: final)" or "末班车 (mòbānchē: the last bus)".

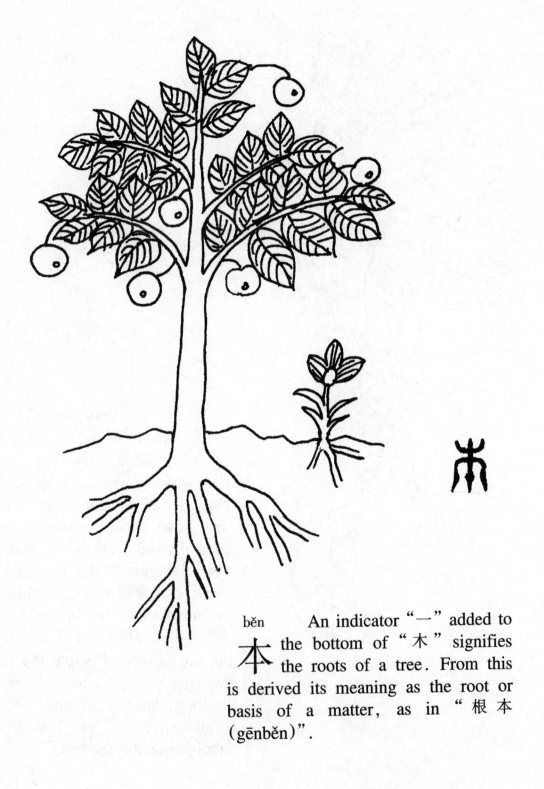

běn 本 An indicator "一" added to the bottom of "木" signifies the roots of a tree. From this is derived its meaning as the root or basis of a matter, as in "根本 (gēnběn)".

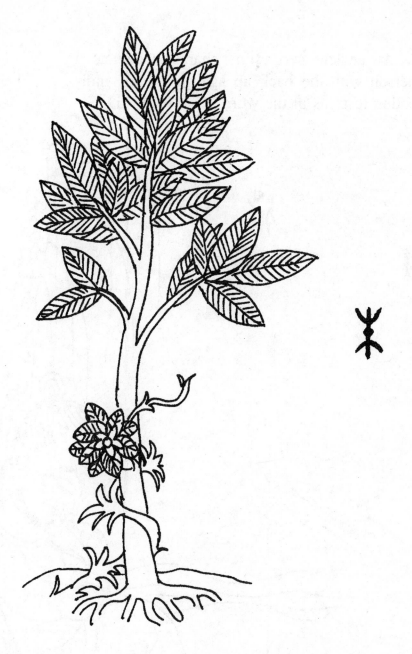

zhū

朱

An indicator " 一 " drawn through the middle of
" 木 " represents a red‑cored cypress tree, and later
came to be used to mean the color of red.

The use of " 朱 " in the popular saying " 近朱者赤, 近墨
者黑(to follow the example of one's company)" indicates
the color of red.

xiū

休 In ancient script this character depicts a person with the back up against a tree, indicating rest, as in the word "休息(xiū·xi)".

xiāng

相

In ancient script, combining "木 (mù: wood)" with "目 (mù: eye)" indicates a blind man's walking stick. As such a stick is used in place of one's eyes to feel out one's way, it means "to look at" or "to watch". In "相亲 (xiāngqīn: mainly in old China, the first time the boy and girl met to see whether the opposite side was an ideal party, might determine the marriage)", "相" means to observe with one's own eyes.

chéng

乘

The ancient form of this character is a front view of a man standing on a tree. "乘" can be found in the idiom "乘风破浪 (chéng fēng pò làng：to brave the wind and the waves)".

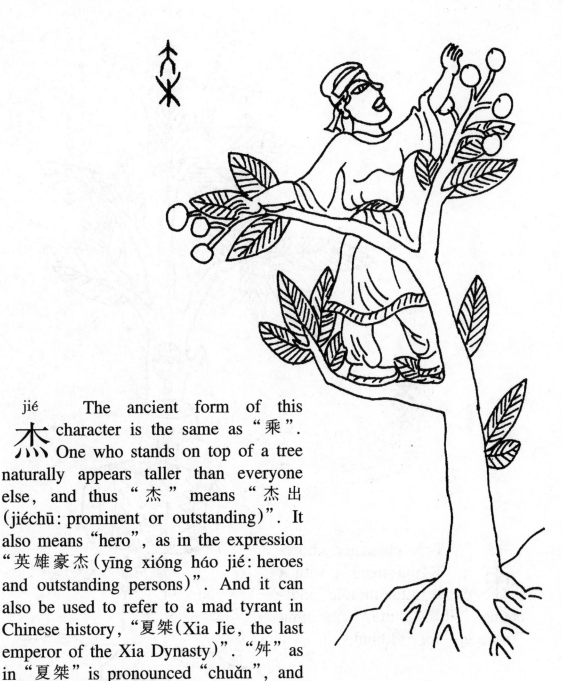

jié
杰
The ancient form of this character is the same as "乘". One who stands on top of a tree naturally appears taller than everyone else, and thus "杰" means "杰出 (jiéchū: prominent or outstanding)". It also means "hero", as in the expression "英雄豪杰 (yīng xióng háo jié: heroes and outstanding persons)". And it can also be used to refer to a mad tyrant in Chinese history, "夏桀 (Xia Jie, the last emperor of the Xia Dynasty)". "舛" as in "夏桀" is pronounced "chuǎn", and depicts the right and left feet.

The traditional form of this character has a "亻" on the left, making "傑". The simplified form is "杰".

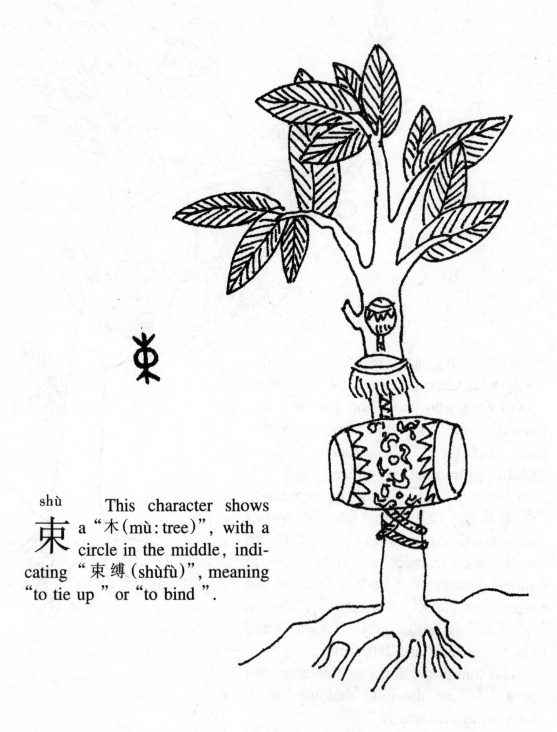

shù

束 This character shows a "木 (mù : tree)", with a circle in the middle, indicating "束缚 (shùfù)", meaning "to tie up" or "to bind".

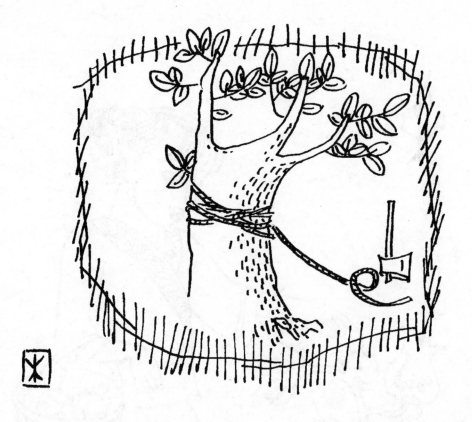

kùn

困

A "木(mù：wood)" written inside "口" signifies and means "捆束 (kǔnshù：tied up)". The popular form of the character was added by a "糸 (mì：representing rope)" to make "綑" and was standardized as "捆"pronounced "kǔn", when unifying the variant forms of Chinese characters after the founding of the People's Republic of China.

Because of being tied up, the character also carries the meaning of suffering or being unable to escape, as in the idiom "困兽犹斗 (kùn shòu yóu dòu：Cornered beasts still fight)". The meaning can be extended to daily life as in "贫困 (pínkùn：impoverishment)", for example, "穷困潦倒 (qióng kùn liǎo dǎo：to live in an impoverished and slipshod way)". The character, when describing physical strength, means " 疲乏 (pífá： weary)", as in the line of verse from *Coal-Vending Old Man* written by Bai Juyi："牛困人饥日已高,市南门外泥中歇。(The hungry man and weary ox see the sun high up in the sky, A rest is taken on the muddy ground to the south of the marketplace.)"

169

采 cǎi   This character depicts a hand (also written as "爪 [zhuǎ : claw]") picking fruit. With the standardization of the writing system "爪" became transformed into "爫".

gǎo

杲 The character is written with "日 (rì: the sun)" on top and "木 (mù: wood)" below, representing the sun shining over treetops. In ancient script, this form means bright. In writings in classical Chinese "杲杲" is often used to describe a scenery with the shining sun, as it is written in *The Book of Songs, Song of Wei State, Bo Xi*: "其雨其雨，杲杲出日。(The bright sun appears while raining.)"

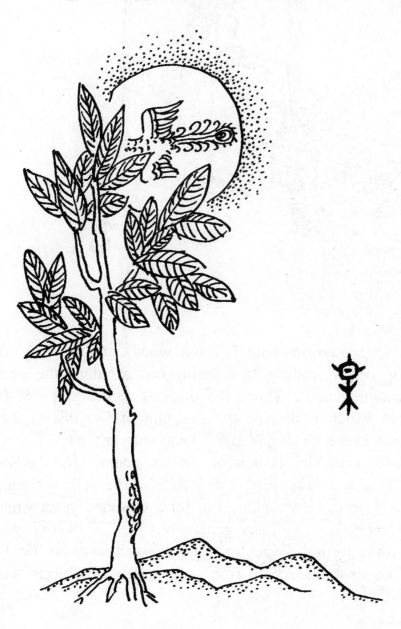

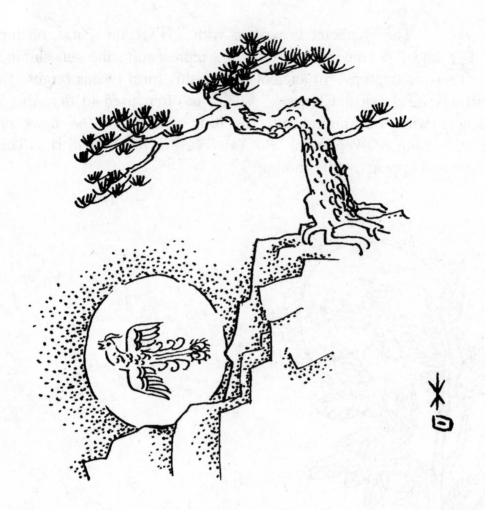

杳 yǎo   The character is written with "木 (mù : wood)" on top and "日 (rì : the sun)" below, indicating a setting sun is behind the trees and it is becoming dark. Thus, the original meaning is "昏暗 (hūn'àn : dim)" from which is derived the meaning of "so distant that nothing is visible", as in the idiom "杳无音信 (yǎo wú yīn xìn)".

The Tang Dynasty poet Cui Hao wrote in his poem, *The Yellow Crane Tower* : "黄鹤一去不复返,白云千载空悠悠。(The yellow crane, once it has gone, will never come again, But for a thousand years white clouds go aimlessly on and on.)" Later generations use "杳如黄鹤 (yǎo rú huáng hè : as far away from the place to which the yellow crane flies)" in comparison to "no news has come from any people or objects that have gone".

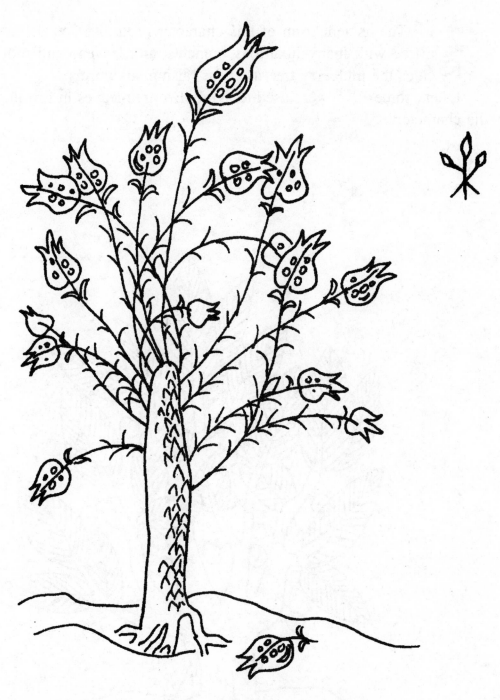

guǒ

果

The ancient form of this character shows the image of a ripe fruit growing on a tree. Later, the top portion was standardized as "田".

sāng   The ancient form of this character protrudes and depicts
桑   a tree with many luxurious branches and leaves, and indicates the mulberry tree used for raising silkworms.

Later, three "又" were used to symbolize tree leaves in forming
the character.

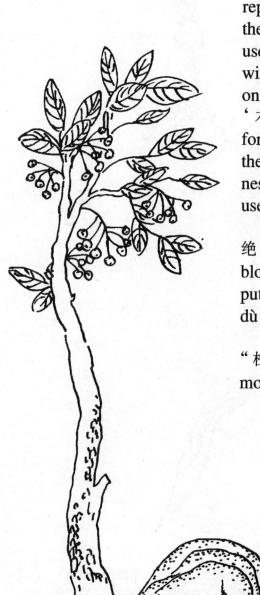

dù   In ancient script, the character 杜 was created with "土 (tǔ: earth)" on either side of "木 (mù: wood)" representing a sort of fruit tree, namely the birchleaf pear. The character, when used on a chop or a seal, was written with "木 (wood)" on top and "土 (earth)" on the bottom. Xu Shen used "杜 (with '木' on the left side)" as the standard form in regulating characters written in the style of *xiao zhuan*, a type of Chinese calligraphy used on seals and still used today.

Later "杜" carries the meaning of "拒绝 (jùjué: to reject)", "阻塞 (zǔsè: to block or obstruct)" as in "杜绝 (dùjué: to put an end to)" and "防微杜渐 (fáng wēi dù jiàn: to check at the outset)".

"Du" is also used as a surname as in "杜甫 (Du Fu)" who is one of China's most reputable poets in history.

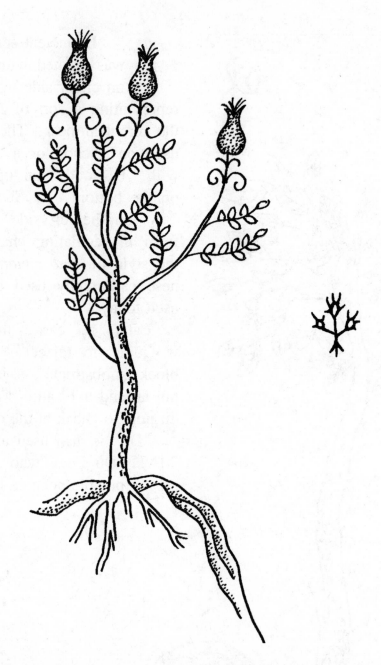

lì
栗   In ancient script, the form resembles woody plant with
burrs on the nut shell, namely "栗子 (lì·zi: chestnut)".
After a change in calligraphy used in official script, the
top part representing the nut was written as "西(xī: west)".

^{sù}
粟　　The character is written with "禾(hé)" representing stalk and leaves in the middle and plum-eared pellets surrounding them. The form in ancient script resembles "粟(pellets)". The hulled pellets are colloquially called millets.

The character is written as "粟" only after a change in calligraphy used in official script.

fēng　　This character originally meant "to plant trees", depicting a right hand planting a sapling in the earth.

The ancient aristocracy, upon receiving an entitlement from the monarch, would proceed to demarcate the boundaries of their territories by planting trees along the borders. These entitled aristocracy became the masters of these lands, which was referred to in ancient books as "封邦建国 (fēng bāng jiàn guó: to confer territory for establishment of a state)" or in short term "enfeoffment".

duì

对

In ancient script, the character resembles a hand （又） holding a sapling growing sturdy represented by "丵" and planting it in the soil.

In ancient times, the nobles planted trees in their manors conferred to them, indicating the demarcation lines and the trees so planted along the borders must grow lushly at a high survival rate. This represented the underlying intention of creating the character.

Later "对" carried the meaning of "答对 (dáduì: to answer a question)" as in the idiom "无言以对 (wú yán yǐ duì: Nothing is said in reply)". The character was and is still used as opposite of "错 (cuò: wrong)", meaning correct.

The traditional form of the character is written as "對".

yì

執

The ancient form of this character depicts a person planting trees or food crops, and means "to plant".

This character was later standardized with "艹" on top, making "蓺", often written as "艺" as in "树艺五谷（shù yì wǔ gǔ：to cultivate the five kinds of grain）".

lín

林 A single tree doesn't make a forest, so two "木 (mù: wood)" are used in ancient script to indicate a stretch of trees.

郁
yù

The ancient form of this character seems to depict a person lying on the ground, with another person using both feet to step on his back. Added by "林（lín: forest）", this character indicates it is taking place in a wild forest. One can well imagine what it is like to run into trouble, be cut off from all help, so "郁" means "郁闷（yùmèn: gloomy）" or "忧郁（yōuyù: depressed）".

The traditional form of writing this character is "鬱".

fán

樊 This character depicts two hands using twigs to weave a fence, and is found in "樊笼 (fánlóng)" and "樊篱 (fánlí)", meaning "cage" and "fence", respectively.

sēn   Ancient writing uses three "木(mù:wood)"
森 to mean many closely packed trees, as in "森林
    (sēnlín:forest)".

yòu

囿 The ancient form of this character shows four "木 (mù: wood)" enclosed in a square, indicating a place where trees flourish, as in "园囿 (yuányòu)", a formal word for "garden".

The standard form of this character consists of a "囗", indicating an enclosed space, such as a garden, and of a "有", which approximates the pronunciation.

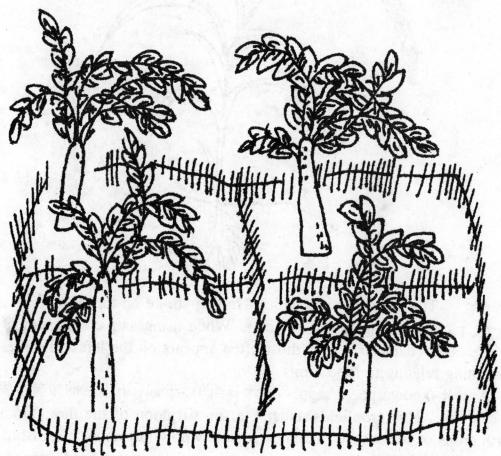

hé　　　This character adds a left-falling stroke on top of a "木", de-
禾　picting a hanging ear of grain. When using as a component of an-
　　other character, "禾" most often appears on the left and represents
something relating to food crops.

　　A well-known poem says: "锄禾日当午,汗滴禾下土。谁知盘中餐,粒
粒皆辛苦。(Hoe cropfields under the sun till noon of the day, Onto the
earth drops of sweat shed, Food on a plate who know about, Hardship fills
every pellet.)" This poem teaches people to value every hard-earned ker-
nel of grain. The character "禾" is used in the original meaning.

nián

年 In ancient script, this character depicts a person carrying stalks of grain (禾) on his shoulder, indicating harvest, as in "年成(nián·cheng)".

In the Temple of Heaven in Beijing there is a hall where the emperor used to come to pray for a bountiful harvest called "祈年殿 (qíniándiàn)".

bǐng 秉 This character depicts a right hand holding a stalk of grain, and means "to grasp or hold", as in "秉烛夜游(bǐng zhú yè yóu: to take an evening stroll with a lantern, a metaphor for making merry)".

The meaning of "秉" has also been extended to mean "to control, preside over", as in "秉公执法(bǐng gōng zhí fǎ: to impartially enforce the law)".

jiān
兼
This character depicts a right hand holding two "禾", or stalks of grain, implying possession of two or more things, as in the expressions "身兼二职（shēn jiān èr zhí: to hold two posts)", and "身兼数职(shēn jiān shù zhí: to hold several posts)".

Because it depicts two "禾", this character can also mean "两倍 (liǎngbèi: double)", as in "昼夜兼程(zhòu yè jiān chéng: to travel day and night)".

cǎo

草   The ancient form of this character resembles the stalks of two newly emerging plants, and means "grass".

As a component of another character, it is written as "艹", which is often referred to as "草头（cǎotóu）or 草字头（cǎozìtóu）", indicating something to do with herbaceous plants.

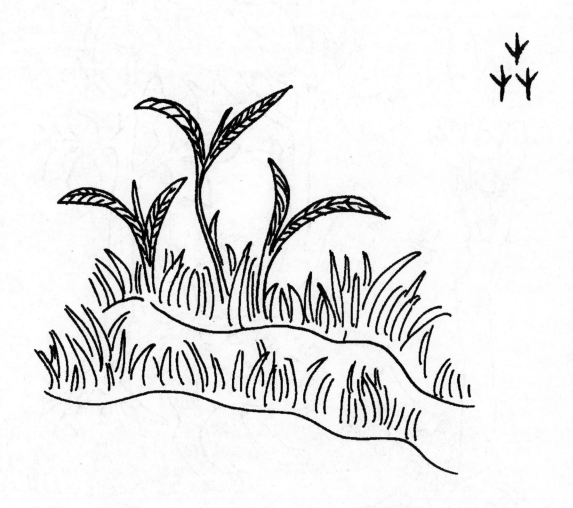

huì   This character originally depicted the stalks of three

卉   sprouting plants, and later came to be written as "卉", and
referred to grass in general. Today, the words "花草
(huācǎo)" and "花卉 (huāhuì)" both mean "flowers and plants",
though now "卉" usually refers to ornamental plants.

mǎng

莽

Ancient script depicts a thick mass of plant stalks to indicate a dense growth of grass, as in the word "莽原（mǎngyuán）", meaning "overgrown wilderness". Later, a "犬" was added, resulting in its modern form.

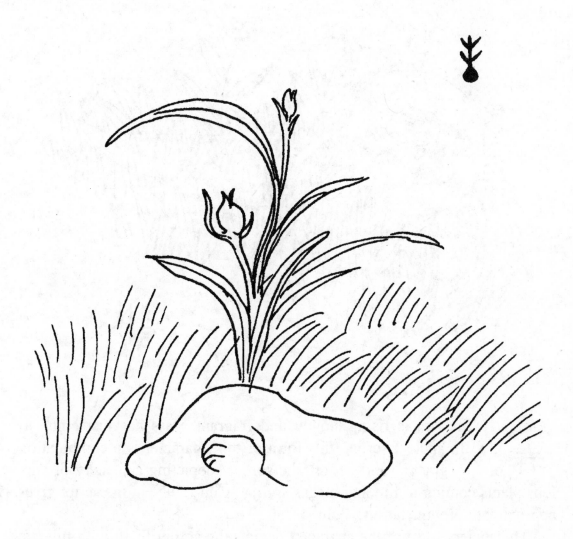

fēng 丰　In ancient script, the form of this character indicates the top portion representing tree saplings while the bottom portion a pile of earth, and means "植树为界 (zhí shù wéi jiè: planting tree to make demarcation lines)". (See separate entry for "封".) From this, the meaning of "枝叶丰茂(zhī yè fēng mào:luxuriant branches and leaves)" or "体态丰满(tǐ tài fēng mǎn:a well filled-out figure)" by extension is derived.

chūn

春

The sun is rising slowly and fragrant grass has just come to life. In ancient script, this form of this character is a combination of "艹(grass)" and "日(rì: the sun)", depicting a scenery of various plants coming to life and means spring again. "屯" in the script gives approximate pronunciation, "tún".

The ancient form of the character depicts the spring filled with full life and therefore, people often compares spring to vigorous life. For example, the great Tang Dynasty poet, Liu Yuxi wrote in his poem *A Toast to The First Meeting With Le Tian in Yangzhou Written at Feast as a Remembrance*: "沉舟侧畔千帆过，病树前头万木春。(By the ship wrecks a thousand sails have passed by, Ahead of dying trees ten thousand trees make spring.)"

Spring Festival, falling between January 1 and 15 on the lunar calendar, is the most significant traditional festival of the Chinese people.

mò

莫 The ancient form of this character sketches the view of a setting sun slowly sinking into the foliage, and meant "dusk".

　　After this character was adopted to mean "not have", a "日 (rì: the sun)" was added below it to indicate its original meaning, and became pronounced "mù", as in "暮色(mùsè:twilight)" and "朝三暮四 (zhāo sān mù sì: this in the morning and that at night or inconsistent, fickle)".

mù

慕

The ancient form of this character is simply a combination of "莫" and "心", meaning "to admire, to envy". "心 (xīn)" indicates something to do with emotions or the mind, and "莫 (mò)" approximates the pronunciation.

In the standard form of writing this character, "心" is written as "小".

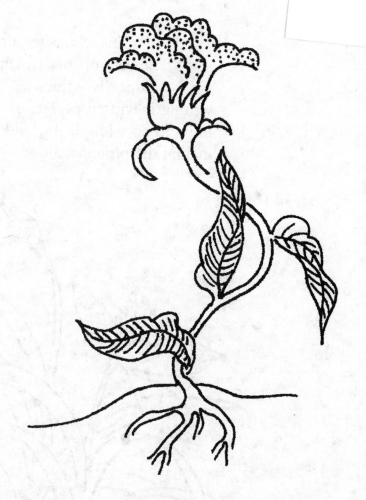

bù

不　　The ancient form of "不" resembles the base of a flower, so ancient people used "杯" to mean a drinking vessel made out of wood which resembles a base of a flower (The variant form is "盂", the component "皿" indicating vessel).

In the classic novel *A Dream of Red Mansions*, the character Dai Yu, in her "葬花辞(*Song of Burying Flowers*)", said: "一抔净土掩风流。(All the talent and romance are covered with a handful of clean earth.)" Here, "抔(póu)" means "to cup with both hands".

"不" later came to indicate the negative. In the modern Chinese language, "不" is pronounced differently under different situations. An individual "不", or when the character following it is pronounced in the first, second or third tone, is pronounced in the fourth tone, as in "不安(bù'ān: unease)", "不行(bùxíng: not work)", "不好(bùhǎo: not good)"; while the character following "不" is pronounced in the fourth tone, it is pronounced in the second tone, as in "不过(bùguò: no more than, but)", "不是(bùshì: not to be)", "不够(bùgòu: not enough)".

197

huā

花 This character originally depicted the flowers of many plants together. It is traditionally written as "華", but in simplified writing is written as "花", "艹" indicating something to do with plants, and "化 (huà)" approximating the pronunciation.

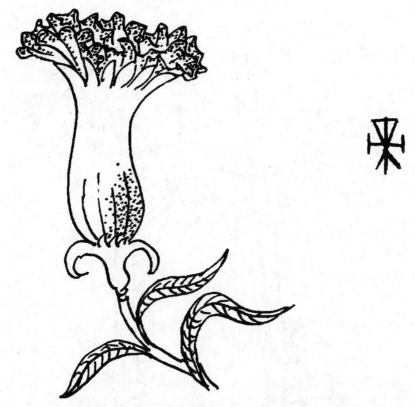

dì

帝

In ancient script, the form of this character appears as the base forming the fundamental part of a flower, and from the meaning, "monarch" is derived by extension. In the eyes of ancient Chinese, the emperor was the dominator overriding everything. The Yellow Emperor and Emperor Yan were the common ancestors in legend respected by various nationalities of China, and until today, descendants of China at home and abroad still call themselves "炎黄子孙 (yán huáng zǐ sūn: sons and grandsons of the Yellow Emperor and Emperor Yan)".

In the year of 221 B.C., Monarch Ying Zheng of the Qin State called himself *Shi Huang Di* and became the first Emperor in China's history, known as Qin Shihuang to the later generations. Ever since that time, "皇帝 (huángdì)" had become the special title for the supreme rulers of the feudal society in China.

Following the adoption of the character as the title of an emperor a "艹" was added to make "蒂 (dì)", carrying the original meaning.

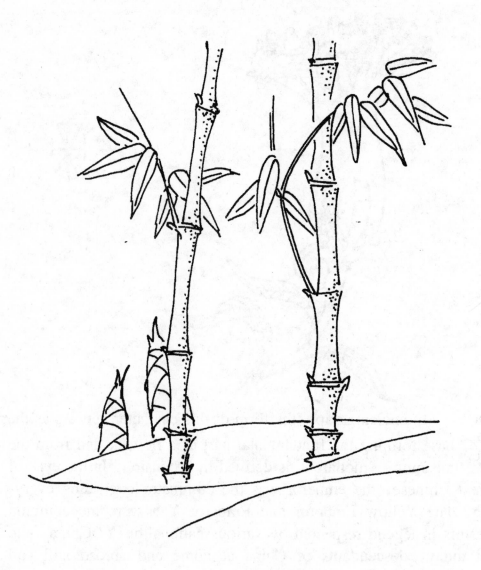

竹

zhú 　　This character depicts the leaves
竹 and branches of two stalks of bamboo,
and thus means "bamboo". The character is standardized "竹", which, as a component of another character, is written as "
竹", commonly called "竹字头 (zhú zì tóu)".

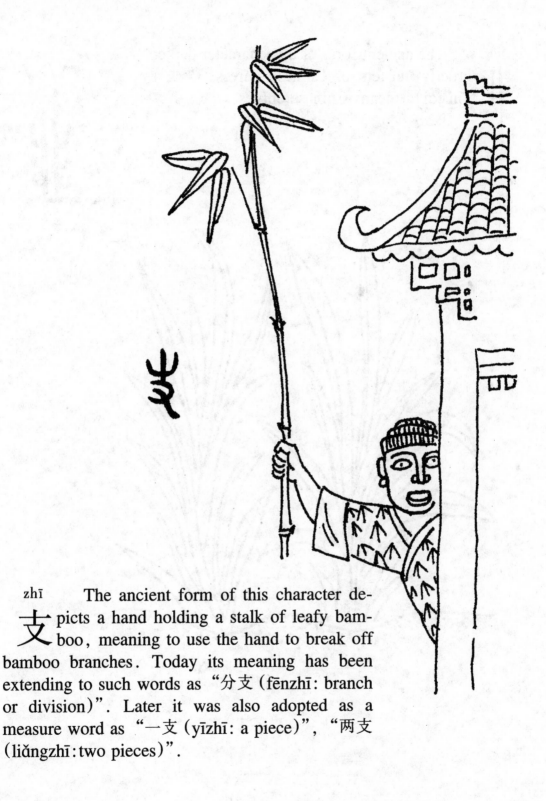

zhī

支 The ancient form of this character depicts a hand holding a stalk of leafy bamboo, meaning to use the hand to break off bamboo branches. Today its meaning has been extending to such words as "分支 (fēnzhī: branch or division)". Later it was also adopted as a measure word as "一支 (yīzhī: a piece)", "两支 (liǎngzhī: two pieces)".

jiǔ   The ancient form of this character depicts
韭   orderly clusters of Chinese chives. "韭菜
     (jiǔcài)" means Chinese chives.

guā

瓜 In ancient script, this character depicts a fruit growing on a vine, thus meaning "melon".

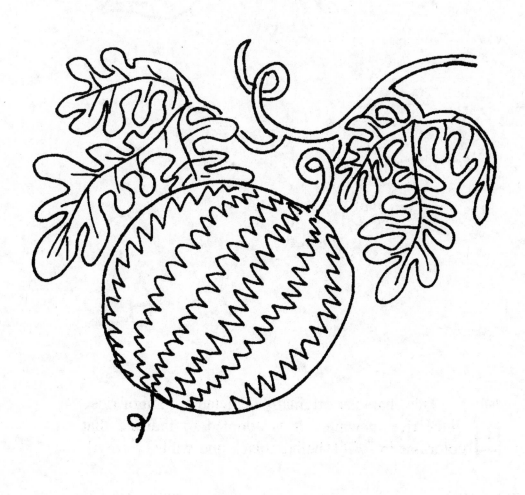

bái   This character originally depicted a grain of rice.
白   Since rice is white, it is adopted to indicate that
color, as in "黑白（hēibái：black and white）".

mǐ   The ancient form of this character indicates rice by depicting many grains of rice. This character appears as a component of other characters, usually on the left or at the bottom, and generally indicates something to do with grain.

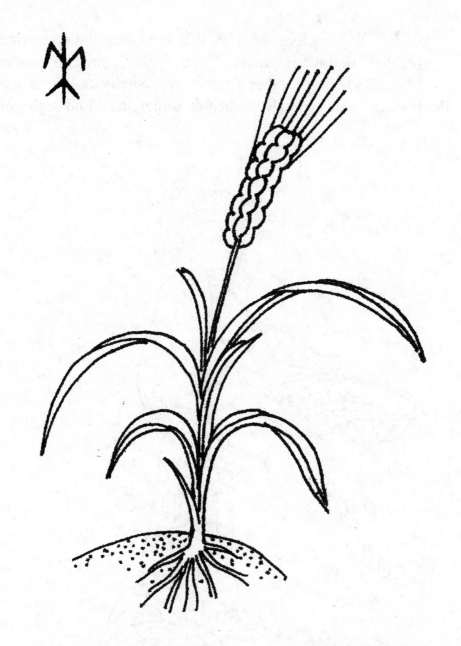

lái   The ancient form of this character depicts a stalk of
来   wheat, and originally did mean "wheat". In ancient China,
people believed that wheat was borne from heaven by birds.
Planted in the fall, it would be harvested the next year. Thus, "来"
means "to come" as in "来往(láiwǎng:to come and go)".

The traditional form of this character is written as "來".

mài 麦   After "来" came to be used as a verb, a "夕", representing a foot, was added underneath "来" to make "麥", thus indicating the planting of wheat in the fall. This character is later simplified to "麦".

qí   The ancient form of this character shows several stalks of
齐   wheat of the same height, meaning "整齐（zhěngqí：orderly)".
The traditional form of this character is written as "齊".

tǔ

In ancient script, this character depicts a lump of earth protruding from the ground, meaning "土地 (tǔdì: earth)", and "泥土 (nítǔ: soil)". Used as a component of other characters, it indicates structures or things made out of earth or stone.

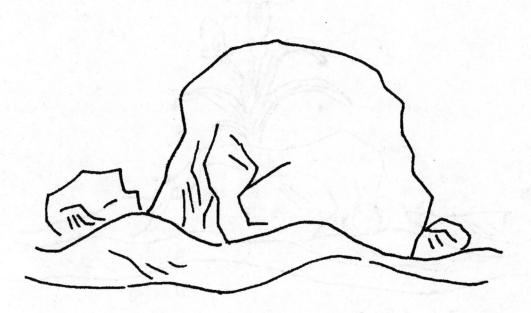

shēng 生   This character represents a small plant written on top of a "土 (tǔ: earth)", indicating "植物生长 (zhí wù shēng zhǎng: the growth of plants)".

tián

田

In ancient script, a "□" indicates a field. A "十" added inside represents the narrow paths between crop fields. Thus, "田" simply means "田地（tiándì：cropland）".

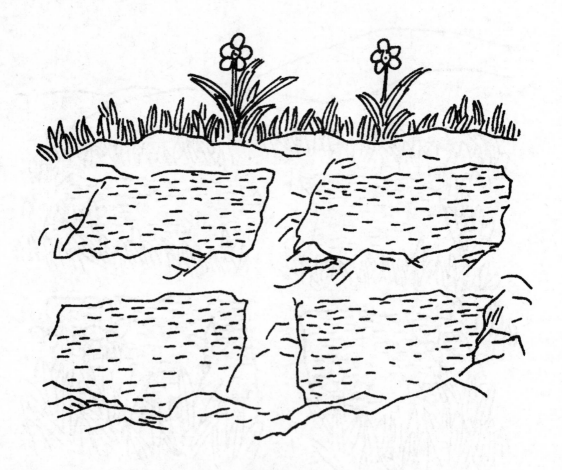

miáo 苗 The plants represented by "艹 (grass)" growing in fields represented by "田 (tián : cropfields)"
are "苗 (crop seedlings)".

bāng

邦　The ancient form of this character appears to be a tree growing on the boundary of a state's manor. This character is found in "封邦建国 (fēng bāng jiàn guó: to confer lands for establishment of a state)". (See the entry for "封 [fēng]").

chóu

畴 The ancient form of this character resembles the twisty furrows made by plowing a field, and is found in the word "田畴 (tiánchóu)" meaning "farmland".

In the modern form of this character, "田" represents the general meaning while "寿 (shòu)" approximates the pronunciation.

shān   This character depicts a group of undulating mountain peaks,
山   and thus means "mountain".
      As a component of another character, "山" usually appears on
the left, top or bottom of a character, and indicates something to do
with mountains or high ground.

qiū　　The ancient form of this character resembles two mountain peaks, and signifies a small mountain or a hill.

fù

阜

The ancient form of "阜" is a "山" turned on end, showing a rocky precipice. Today it means "mound".

When acting as a component of another character, it is written on the left as "阝", and indicates something to do with mountains or terrain.

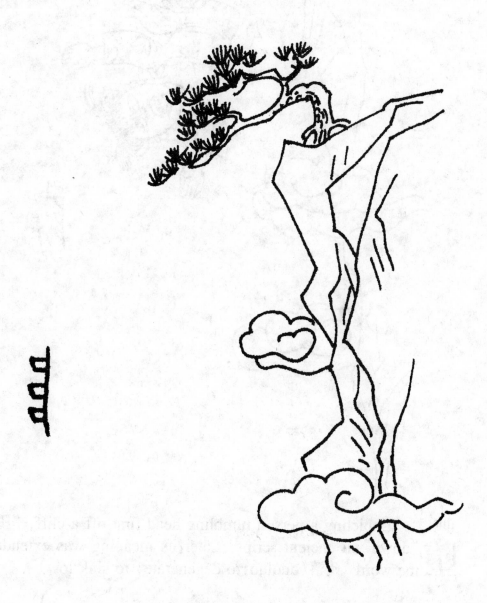

duò

堕 Depicting a person tumbling head first off a cliff, "堕" means "down" in ancient script. Later its meaning was extended, as in the word "堕落(duòluò：to degenerate, to sink low)".

zhì
陟

The ancient form of this character depicts two feet ascending a mountain, meaning "登 (dēng: to climb)", or "攀登 (pāndēng: to scale)".

There is a line from *The Book of Songs* which reads: "陟彼高岗 (zhì bǐ gāo gāng)", expressing a scene out of the wife's imagination in which the husband is ascending a lofty mountain.

jiàng

降

Two feet heading down a mountain was the ancient form of "降", which meant "to come down from a high place". In modern Chinese, "降" means "to descend".

líng 陵   In ancient script, this character depicts a person with one foot on flat ground, one foot on some rocks. Therefore, its original meaning was "to scale". Later, the meaning of "陵" was extended to mean a large pile of earth, such as "陵墓 (língmù: a burial mound)", and the character "凌 (líng)" was used to mean "攀登 (pāndēng: to scale)". The famous poet Du Fu, in his poem "望岳 (*Watching Mount Tai*)" wrote: "会当凌绝顶,一览众山小。(When one ascends the mountain peak, All the mountains look small.)"

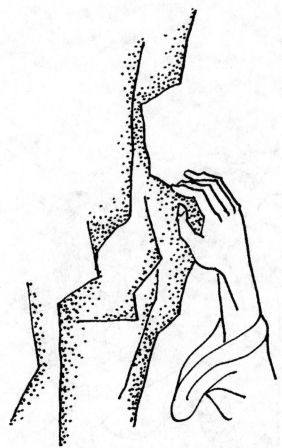

fǎn

反

The component "厂" in "反" represents both a mountain and a left hand. In ancient script, the character signifies ascending a mountain cliff by hand.

The character also means "翻转 (fānzhuǎn)" or "覆 (fù)" signifying "to turn over". An example from *The Book of Songs, Section Zhou Nan, Guan Ju* says: "辗转反侧,寤寐思服。(Tossing and turning in bed, Consider over and again whether awakened or asleep.)" Other examples are such idioms as "易如反掌(yì rú fǎn zhǎng: as easy as turning the hand over)", "反戈一击(fǎn gē yī jī: to turn one's weapon around and strike those he formerly sided with)". The character also carries the meaning "相反(xiāngfǎn: to the contrary)" as in the idiom "适得其反(shì dé qí fǎn: contrary to the desired outcome)".

shí

石

The ancient form of this character depicts a rock positioned at the bottom of a cliff. It means "rock" as in "石头 (shí·tou)" or "石块(shíkuài)".

As a component of another character, "石" indicates something to do with stones, earthen or stone buildings and tools.

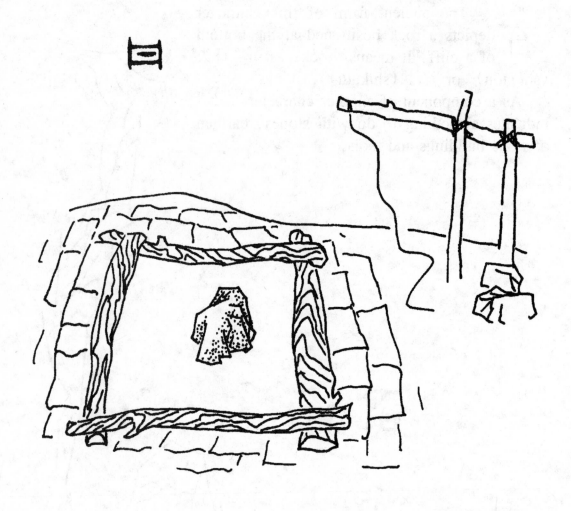

dān

丹

The ancient form of this character depicts a chunk of a kind of ore in the mouth of a hole and, if used for making dye, is called "朱砂(zhūshā∶cinnabar)".

Because cinnabar is red, "丹" is therefore used to mean that color. The hero Wen Tianxiang, before his death, wrote the immortal lines "人生自古谁无死,留取丹心照汗青(Death has happened to everyone since ancient times, Let my loyal heart shine in the pages of history）", expressing the martyr spirit of the poet.

青
qīng   The top half of the ancient form of this character shows a "生 (shēng)", representing a sprouting plant, while the bottom half depicts a mine pit indicating extraction from the mineral of the color of plants, called "青色(qīngsè:green or blue)".

In addition, blue can also be extracted from indigo plants. An ancient Chinese philosopher, Xun Zi, noted in his book "劝学篇 (*Encourage Learning*)": "青,取之于蓝而青于蓝。(Blue comes from the indigo plant but is bluer than the plant it comes from.)"

yù　　The ancient form of this character resembles a string of valuable stones, and means "jade".

　　In ancient script, it is very difficult to distinguish "玉" and
"王 (wáng)". To tell them apart, a dot is added to make "玉". As a
component of another character, it is written as "⺩" or "王", indicating something to do with precious stones.

nòng　　This character originally depicted two hands
弄　playing with a piece of jade, meaning "玩弄
(wánnòng：to play with)".

jué

珏

The ancient form of this character depicts two strings of precious stones. Ancient people used tiny pieces of jade or shells as money. Because pieces of jade are fairly tiny, thread is used to string them together. "珏" was an ancient commercial practice reflected truly in ancient script.

In modern Chinese, "珏" is used mostly in the names of people or places, such as the character in the famous contemporary novel *Family*, Ruijue.

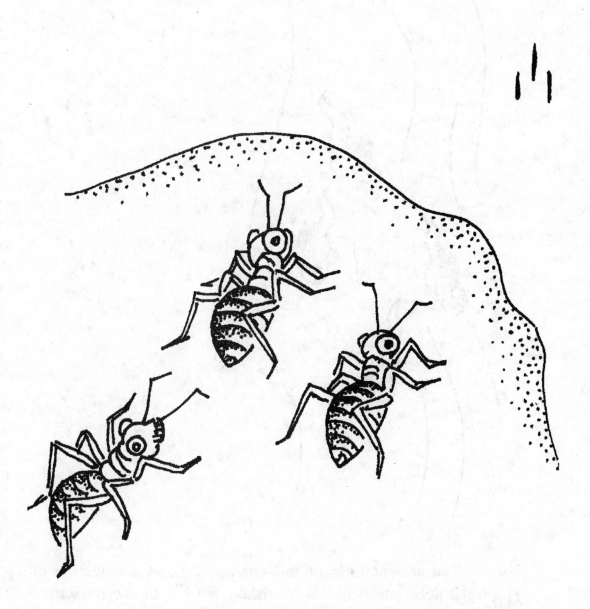

xiǎo   The original form of this character uses
小   several small dots to represent "small".

shǎo The ancient form of this character shows a scattering of
少 small dots, meaning "稀少(xīshǎo：few)". In ancient script,
the difference between "少" and "小" is that "少" is represented by four dots whereas "小" is represented by only three.

Later，"少" also came to be pronounced "shào", meaning
"young".

水 shuǐ　　In ancient script this character depicts a watercourse in the middle, with drops of water on both sides, thus meaning "water". As a component of another character, it is often written as " 氵", or " 水", indicating something to do with water.

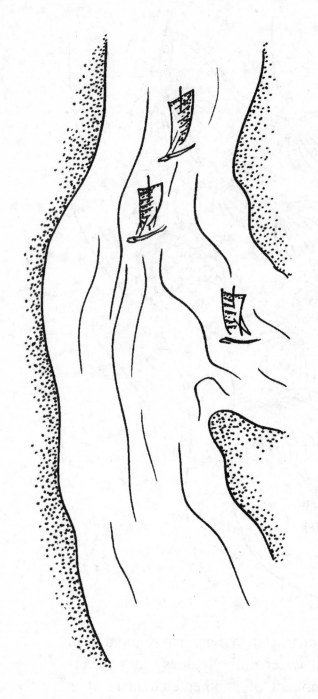

伱

pài
派   The ancient script indicates a river flows in divided courses and means tributaries. Chairman Mao Zedong wrote in his poem *Yellow Crane Tower* (*to the tune of Pu Sa Man*): "茫茫九派流中国，沉沉一线穿南北。(Wide, wide flow the nine streams through the land, Dark, dark threads the line from south to north.)" Here "九派 (jiǔpài)" refers to the numerous tributaries of the Yangtze River.

From the tributaries, the meaning of the character is extended to "派别 (pàibié: schools)", "派生 (pàishēng: derive)".

shè

涉

Two feet on either side of water indicates "to wade", as in "涉水过河（shè shuǐ guò hé: to wade through a river）". The "涉" in the idiom "跋山涉水（bá shān shè shuǐ: to travel by climbing up hills and wading over rivers）" retains its original meaning.

fú

浮

The ancient form of this character shows a hand grabbing the head of a child who has fallen in the water, making it float on the surface of the water, as in the word " 浮 (to float)".

shǔ "黍", or millet, was the principle crop of the Shang Dy-
黍 nasty. In bumper years, the Shang people would use leftover
millet to make wine. Therefore, the ancient form of "黍" is
composed of a ripe "禾(hé：ear of grain)" and "水(shuǐ：water)".

shā
沙

This character depicts small grains in the middle of water, meaning "sand", as in "沙子(shā·zi)".

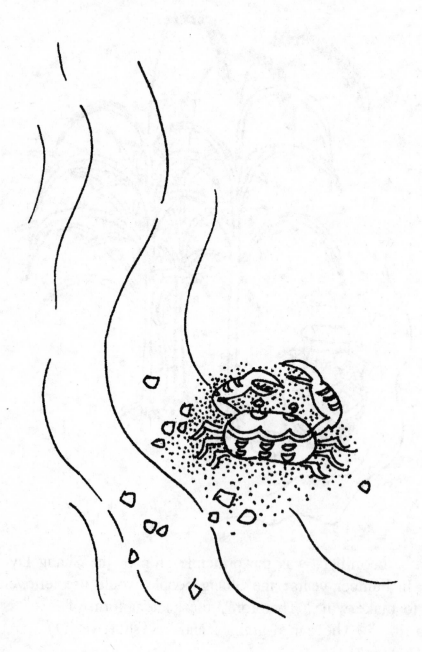

chuān

川 The ancient form of this character depicts a stream flowing down amid a mountain. It is found in the word "山川 (shānchuān: mountains and rivers)".

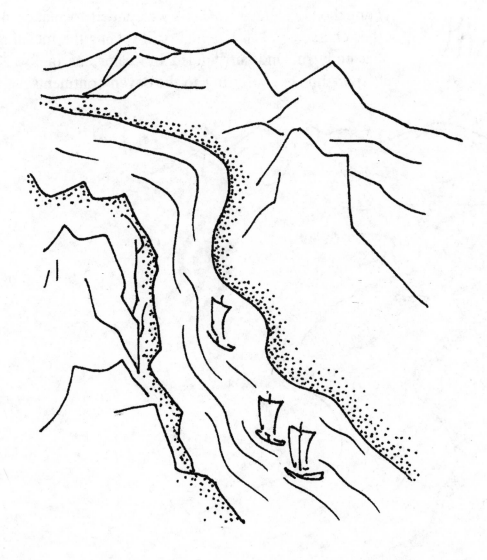

zhōu

州

This character originally depicted a piece of land surrounded by water, and meant "small island". There is a line in the opening section of *The Book of Songs* which reads: "关关雎鸠,在河之洲(On an islet in a river, A pair of turtle-doves are cooing)", wherein "洲" carries just this meaning.

After "州" was borrowed to indicate an administrative division (as in "苏州 [sūzhōu]" and "杭州 [hángzhōu]", etc.), a "氵" was added to make another character, "洲", which still retains the meaning of a body of land surrounded by water, as in "七大洲(qīdàzhōu)", referring to the seven continents.

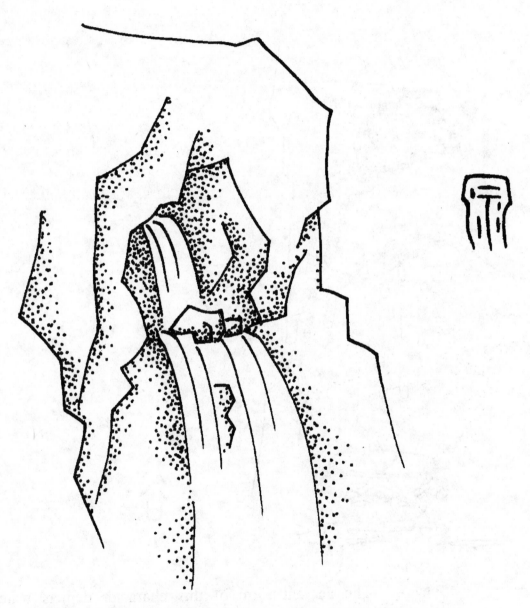

quán

泉 With its ancient form depicting water flowing out of a mountain cave, "泉" means "spring".

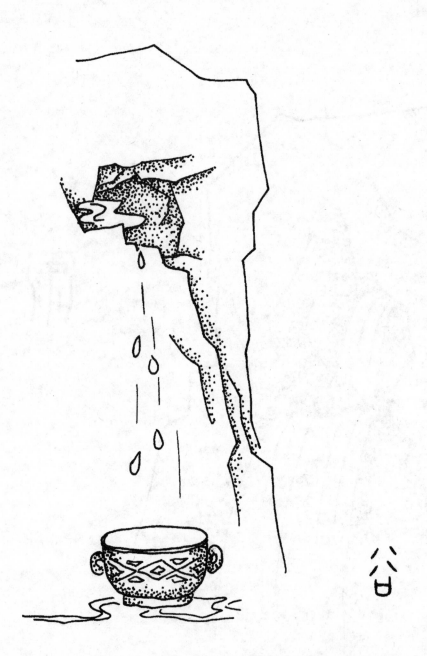

谷 gǔ   The ancient form of this character depicts water which has just flown out of a wellspring and has not yet formed into a stream. It is found in the word "山谷(shāngǔ)", meaning "valley, gorge".

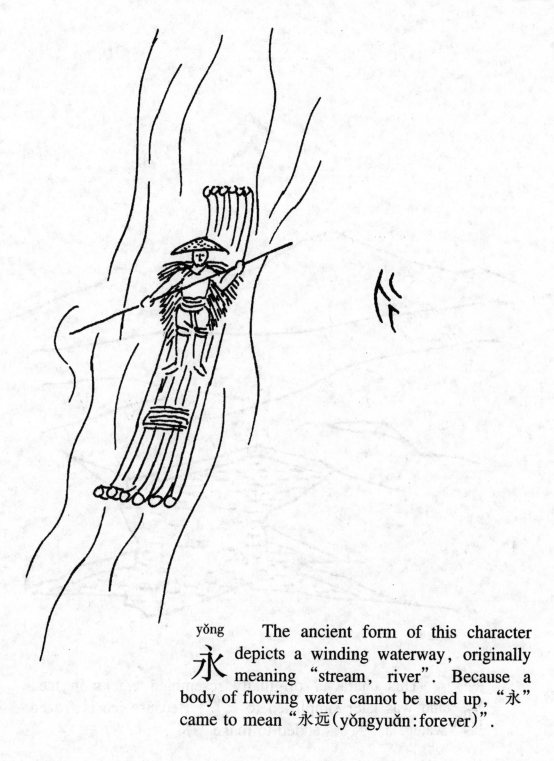

yǒng   The ancient form of this character
永   depicts a winding waterway, originally
meaning "stream, river". Because a
body of flowing water cannot be used up, "永"
came to mean "永远(yǒngyuǎn:forever)".

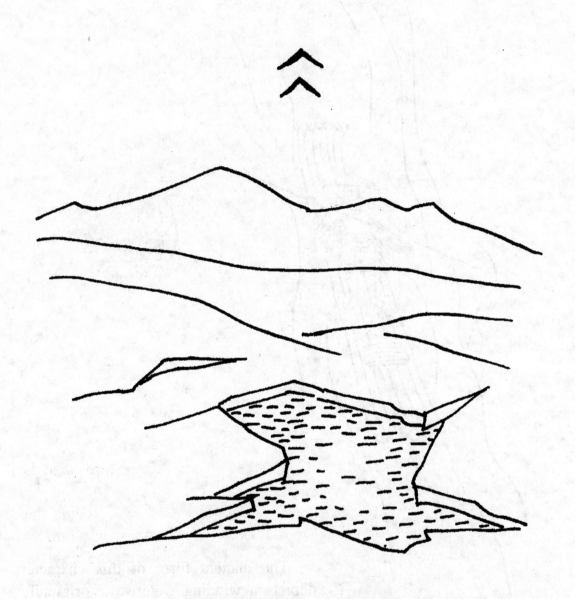

bīng 冰   This character originally resembled cracks in ice, and was later simplified to "冫". Because ice is frozen water, a "水" is added to make "冰".

niǎo   This character originally depicted a long‑tailed bird, and is

鸟   written traditionally as "鳥".

    The Book of Songs says："天命玄鸟，降而生商，"telling the mythical story of how the Shang Dynasty sprang from a heavenly bird.

    As a component of another character，"鸟" appears on the right or bottom，and mainly indicates animals that can fly，such as "鹦鹉 (yīngwǔ: parrot)"，"鸳鸯 (yuān·yāng: mandarin duck)" and so on. Though "鸭 (yā: duck)" and "鹅 (é: goose)" are not good at flying，by reviewing their physiological structures and changes in the ecological environment，we can trace their origins to also being birds. The traditional form is "鳥"，and it has been shortened to "鸟".

míng

鸣 The ancient form of this character depicts a bird with a protruding mouth, symbolizing the call of a bird.

Later, "鸣" is extended to indicate any sort of sound occurring in nature.

244

wěi
唯　The ancient form of the character is a combination of "口" and "隹", meaning the cry of bird. Later the character was borrowed to mean respect and obedience as in the idiom "唯唯诺诺(wěi wěi nuò nuò：to be absolutely obedient)".

　　"唯" is also pronounced "wéi" in the second tone, meaning "单单(dāndān：alone)", "只(zhǐ：only)", as in "唯一(wéiyī：the only one)", "唯物主义(wéi wù zhǔ yì：materialism)", etc.

wū
乌
The difference between "乌" and "鸟" is that "鸟" has an eye drawn in while "乌" does not. "乌" depicts a bird covered in long, black feathers, making it impossible to see the eye, as found in the word "乌鸦 (wūyā)", meaning "crow".

The Tang Dynasty poet Zhang Jizeng used the following lines of verse to describe an evening view from Hanshan Temple outside of Suzhou: "月落乌啼霜满天,江枫渔火对愁眠。(The sky is full of frost with setting moon and crying crows, Feeling grieved in sleep are the maples trees on the river bank and the fire on fishing boats.)" Here "乌" means "乌鸦(crows)".

246

zhuī

隹

This character originally depicted the form of a bird. The difference between "隹" and "鸟" is that "鸟" is shown with wings while "隹" is not.

Later, "隹" came to be used in other characters to approximate pronunciation, as in "椎 (zhuī: vertebra)", "锥 (zhuī: awl)", "维 (wéi: to tie up, hold together)" and "唯 (wéi: only, alone)".

zhī

只

This character originally showed a right hand holding a bird（隹）, and is a measure word, as in "一只（yīzhī: one piece）", "两只（liǎngzhī: two pieces）", etc.

The traditional form of this character is written as "隻".

shuāng   The traditional form of this character depicts a right hand
双 (represented by "又") holding two birds (represented by
"隹"), meaning "一双(yīshuāng：a pair)".
The traditional form of this character is written as "雙".

雀　què　This character is formed by the components "小 (xiǎo: small)" and "隹 (zhuī: bird)", indicating a small bird, such as "麻雀(máquè: a sparrow)".

_{jìn}

进

The ancient form of this character shows a "隹" underneath a "止", and means "to hunt bird and fowl". Its meaning was later extended to mean "进(to advance or to enter)".

In the traditional form of writing, "止" is written as "辶", thus transforming this character into "進". In the simplified form, "井 (jǐng)" approximates the pronunciation.

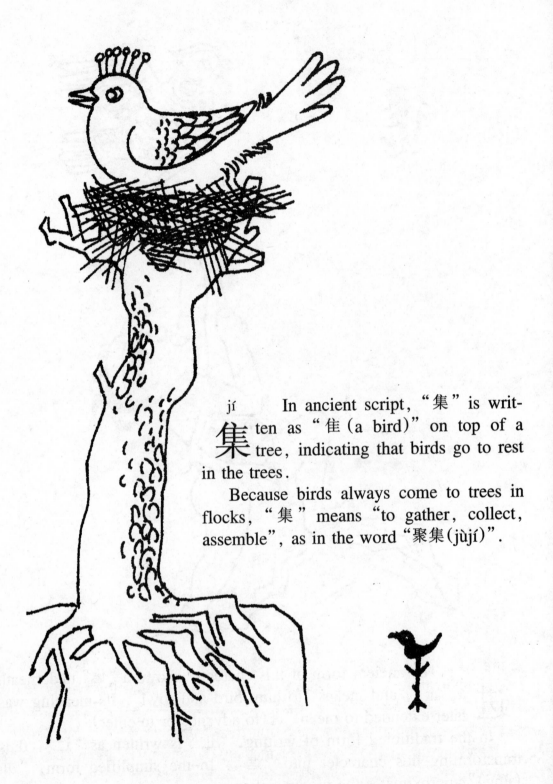

jí   In ancient script, "集" is written as "隹 (a bird)" on top of a
tree, indicating that birds go to rest
in the trees.

Because birds always come to trees in
flocks, "集" means "to gather, collect,
assemble", as in the word "聚集 (jùjí)".

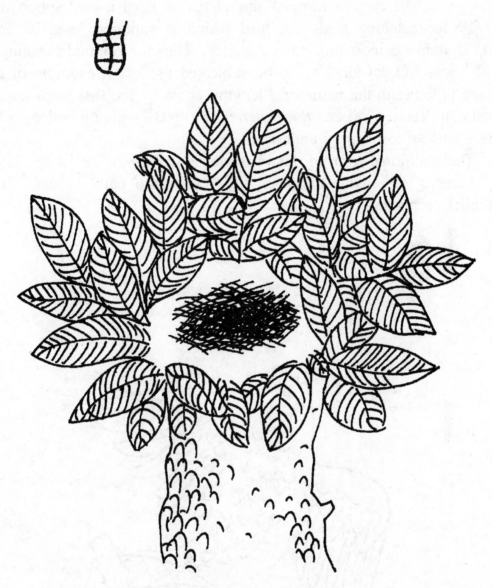

xī
西 This character originally resembled a bird's nest, indicating that "鸟在树上栖息 (Birds roost in the trees)".

The traditional form of the character is written as "棲": "木 (mù)" indicating a tree, and "妻 (qī)" approximating the pronunciation. This was later simplified to "栖 (qī)", with "西" now acting as the pronunciation component and expressing the meaning.

Birds come to their nests as the sun is setting in the west, so this character is also borrowed to indicate the direction "west".

lí The ancient form of this character is of a contraption used for catching birds. A bird which is captured loses its freedom—a most unfortunate matter. Thus the original meaning of "离" was "遭受(zāoshòu: to be subjected to)". An example of this usage is found in the name of a lengthy poem by the first great ancient poet Qu Yuan, "离骚(*Encountering Sorrow*)", giving voice to the great internal torment he underwent.

The traditional form of this character is written as "離".

Later, "离" came to mean "离别(líbié: to part)", and "分离(fēnlí: to separate)".

254

yàn   The ancient form of this character
燕 depicts a complete bird, including the
head, feet, wings, and body. It means
"swallow (a kind of bird)".

Ancient legend held that the people of the
Shang Dynasty were descended from a swallow. Therefore, the Shang regarded the swallow as their original ancestor, and created the character "燕" to specially denote the sacredness of this bird.

guān

观   The ancient form of the character protrudes the two large eyes of an owl, and means "to watch or observe". The ancient form of this character was written as "雚", and later "見" was added to make "觀", emphasizing the original meaning.

"雚" may approximate the pronunciation. For example, the component "氵" is added to make "灌", meaning to water the farmland while the component "缶" is added to make "罐 (a vessel)", both characters are pronounced "guàn" in the fourth tone. Besides, "欠" may also be added by "雚" to make "歡", pronounced "huān", meaning to feel pleasant and happy, or "木" added to make "權", pronounced "quán", representing an ancient plant and now representing in most cases right or power; in the latter two characters, "雚" is simplified to "又" to make "欢" and "权".

jī The ancient character resembles a
鸡 chicken, and later, "奚" pronounced
"xī" is added to retain the original
meaning "chicken". The traditional form of
the character is written as "雞".

fēi   In ancient script, this character depicts a bird spreading its wings and
taking flight, meaning "to fly".

The traditional form of this character is
written as "飛".

yǔ   This character resembles two feathers or in-
羽 sect wings, and means "feather", as in the
word "羽毛(yǔmáo)".

luǎn   The ancient form of this character depicts the testi-
卵   cles, commonly called ovum. Because it relates to re-
production, this character later came to be used to refer
to the eggs of birds, fish, and insects.

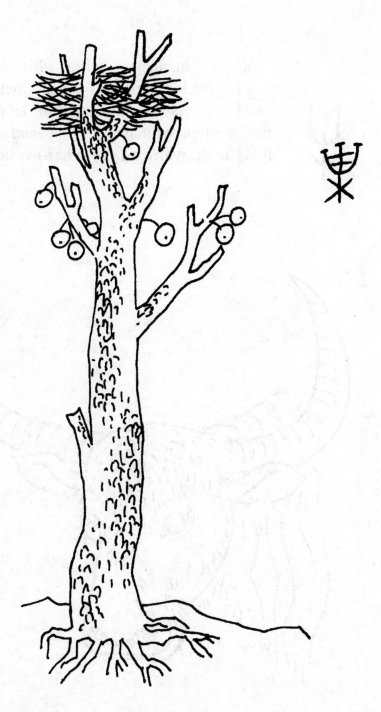

cháo

巢   The ancient form of this character depicts a bird's nest in a tree.

niú   In ancient script, this character depicts the long horns of a bull, meaning "cow".

As a component of another character, this is often written as "牜", and indicates something to do with cows or other livestock.

mǔ

牡

"⊥" represented male genitals, and later, it was written as "士"; and "牛(cow)" referred to, in general, any animals. The ancient form of this character is a combination of "牛" and "⊥", meaning male animal. *The Book of Songs, Song of Bei State* says: "雉鸣求其牡 (A chirping pheasant is asking to mate a male one)", and here the original meaning is used.

"牡" is used very often in names of flowers as in "牡丹(mǔdān: peony)". Ancient people

thought the peony was the crown of flowers because of its ethereal color and celestial fragrance. In the past, it was not named a peony. This flower is called "Tian Peng" or Chinese herbaceous peony in the Shu (present Sichuan Province), and was initially named in the prosperous Tang Dynasty. Legend says that Empress Wu Zetian issued an imperial edict ordering all peonies in Luoyang to be in full bloom in one night. The territory of Shu in the period of Three Kingdoms, Chang'an, the capital of the Tang Dynasty and Luoyang during the Song Dynasty are places where peonies were once in bloom. It is said: "唯有牡丹真国色,花开时节动京城。(The peony alone makes merit of reigning beauty, its flowers when in bloom cause a sensation throughout the capital.)" Nowadays, peonies in Luoyang are still so attractive that guests and friends from all parts of the country and the world come to see them.

pìn

牝

"匕" in ancient script represents female; a combination of "匕" with such other words as "豕（shǐ: pig）", "虎（hǔ: tiger）", "马（mǎ: horse）", "羊（yáng: sheep）" or "牛（niú: cow）" represented various female animals. Later, the component "牛（cow）" was used to represent all animals. Hence, the character "牝".

mù The ancient form of this character depicts a person using
牧 a stick to drive a cow. It means to put cows or sheep out to
pasture or to herd them together, and later came to apply to
all kinds of domestic animals.

jiǎo

角 This character originally depicts the horn of a cow, but later is extended to refer to the horns of any animal.

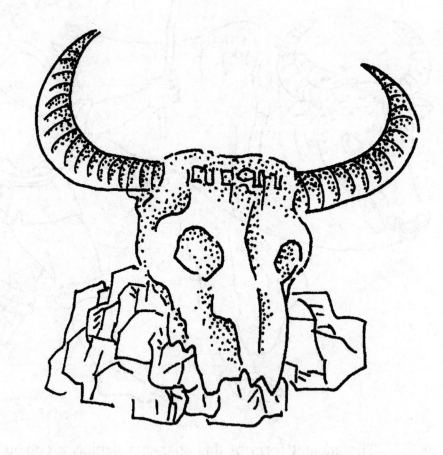

jiě

解

The ancient form of this character depicts two hands removing the horns of a cow, and means to carve up the body of an animal.

Later, the original "手" component was transformed into a "刀", making "解". Now, "解" has various meanings, as in such words as "分解（fēnjiě: to decompose）", "解除（jiěchú: to remove something from…）", "解释（jiěshì: interpretation）", and "了解（liǎojiě: to understand）".

yáng   This character, meaning "sheep", is a de-
羊 piction of a sheep's head.

shān 膻   The ancient form of the character is three sheep put together, signifying a crowd of sheep which gave the smell of mutton, hence the meaning of the word.

The character is later written as "膻" and the component "亶" approximates the pronunciation while "月（肉月）", gives the meaning.

qiāng

羌   The ancient form of this character depicts a sheep's head atop the figure of a person, referring to shepherding people of ancient China, the Qiang.

In a verse from "出塞(*Go Beyond the Great Wall*)" by the Tang poet Wang Zhihuan: "羌笛何须怨杨柳,春风不度玉门关。(The Qiangs need not complain about poplar and willow, For the spring breeze will not come over the Yumen Pass.)" "羌" refers to the Qiang people.

The Qiang people are still around today, living in Sichuan Province, southwestern China.

270

xiū

羞   In ancient script, this character depicts a hand grabbing the head of a sheep, and signifies something good to eat.

       Later, "羞" was borrowed to express embarrassment or shyness. The original meaning is signified by adding a "饣"to make "馐(xiū)", meaning "delicacy".

shǐ   The ancient form of this character depicts the sideview of
豕   a pig, and thus means "pig".

      In modern Chinese, "豕" can only be found in an idiom,
"狼奔豕突 (láng bēn shǐ tū: to run like wolves and rush like boars)".

      "豕" was gradually replaced by the character "豬", later written
as "猪 (zhū)".

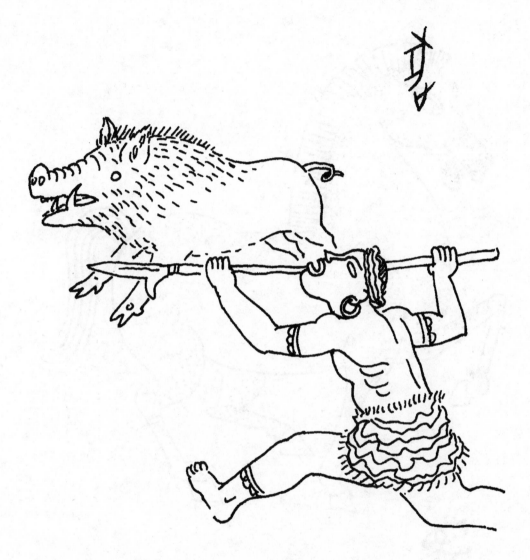

zhú   A "止", signifying a foot, drawn below a "豕 (a pig)",
逐 signifies pursuit of some wild boar. "夸父逐日 (kuā fù zhú rì)"
from the classic work "山海经 (*Book on Mountains and Rivers*)" written in ancient China, records the moving tale of Kua Fu's pursuit of the sun.

The component "止" is standardized as "辶", as shown in the head character.

mǎ   This character is a depiction of a horse.
马   The traditional form is written as "馬", and later became simplified to "马" through the cursive calligraphy style. Used as a component of another character, it signifies things having to do with horses or other animals similar to horses.

yù

驭

This character originally depicted a hand wielding a whip and driving a horse. It is found in the word "驾驭 (jiàyù)" meaning "to drive（a horse, etc.）". The "又" component signifies a hand.

jià The ancient form of this character depicts a hand
驾 holding a whip and an open mouth, both urging on a
horse. This character is found in the word "驾驭
(jiàyù)" meaning "to drive (a horse, etc.)".

quǎn In ancient script, this character shows the form of a dog
犬 with a curled tail. As a component of another character, this
character appears as "犭" or "犬", signifying something to do
with dogs or animals in general.

chòu

臭   As a dog has keen sense of smell, the character in ancient script is a combination of a "自(zì:oneself)" representing the nose and a "犬(quǎn:dog)" meaning "to smell". Thus, the character "臭", originally pronounced "xiù", means smelling, as in "无声无臭(wú shēng wú xiù: without sound and smell, unknown)" recorded in *The Book of Songs, Section Da Ya, Emperor Wen*.

Classic writing says, "其臭如兰(qí xiù rú lán:smell as orchid)", here "臭" means a pleasant smell. Later, this character was borrowed to mean smelly, opposite to fragrant, so the initial meaning is indicated by adding a "口(mouth)" to "臭(smell)" making "嗅(xiù)".

278

xiàng

象

The ancient form of this character is a depiction of a sideview of an elephant.

In ancient times, elephants flourished in the central plains of China and thus another name for Henan Province is "豫(yù)", with "予(yù)" providing the pronunciation.

为　　This character originally depicted a hand leading an elephant along, as if training it or using it. It can mean "有所
作为(yǒu suǒ zuò wéi：Something can be accomplished)".

The traditional form of writing this character is "為", and is
simplified to "为" through the cursive calligraphy style.

hǔ

虎 Meaning tiger, this character resembles the sideview of that beast. When used as a component of another character, it is written as "虍", and usually indicates the pronunciation.

lù

鹿   This character, meaning "deer", is a depiction of a deer from the side. "鹿" and "禄(official salary in ancient times)" have the same pronunciation. The coat of a deer is quite beautiful. For these reasons, ancient people took the deer as a symbol of good fortune.

qìng

庆 Ancient people often presented a deerskin as a means of expressing congratulations. Therefore, the ancient form of "庆" consists of a "鹿(lù:deer)", a "心(xīn:heart)" and a "夊(xī: signifying 'foot')", resulting in "慶". This character illustrates presentation of both good intentions and a beautiful deerskin to express congratulations and blessings.

The simplified form of this character is written as "庆".

lù   This character depicts a deer running in a forest,
麓   and refers to the forested area at the base of a mountain. The component "鹿" helps express the meaning
as well as provide the pronunciation.

tù

兔 The ancient form of this character is a depiction of a rabbit, and takes on this meaning.

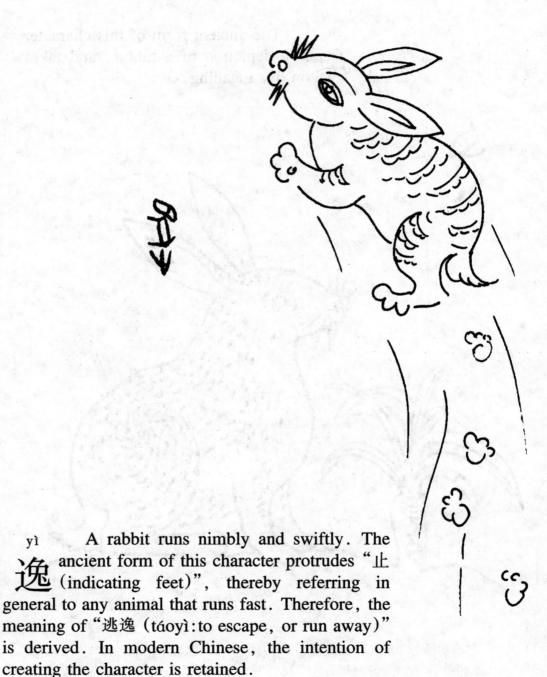

yì 逸 　A rabbit runs nimbly and swiftly. The ancient form of this character protrudes "止 (indicating feet)", thereby referring in general to any animal that runs fast. Therefore, the meaning of "逃逸 (táoyì：to escape, or run away）" is derived. In modern Chinese, the intention of creating the character is retained.

shǔ 　　Meaning "老鼠(lǎoshǔ:rat)", this char-
鼠　acter originally depicted that animal's protruding teeth.

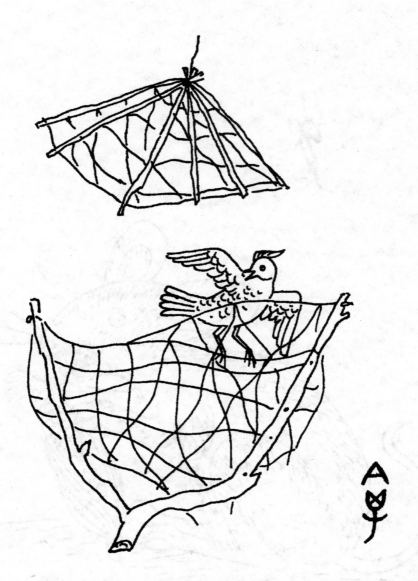

qín

禽

The top half of the ancient form of this character depicts a kind of covering, while the bottom half depicts a kind of net used for catching birds or beasts. A covering and a net, when used together, signify a trap from which there is no escape. Thus the word "擒(qín)", meaning "to capture, catch". When "禽" came to mean "fowl", as in "飞禽走兽(fēi qín zǒu shòu: flying birds and running beasts)", a "扌" was added to make "擒".

wàn
万
This character originally depicted a scorpion, and was written as "萬". By adopting the cursive calligraphy form, this character is later simplified to "万".

Because scorpions and their holes are quite numerous, "万" was later borrowed to signify a great number, as in "亿万 (yìwàn: hundreds of millions)".

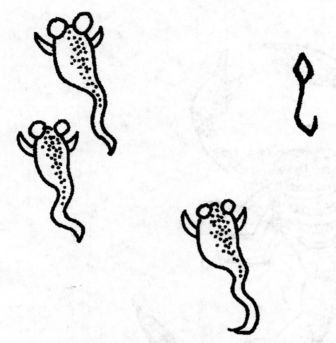

chóng   This character originally depicted three tiny insects.

虫   In *The Book of Rites* written during the West Han Dynasty, it says: "The best of the fur beasts is *qilin* or (Chinese) unicorn. The best of the feather beasts is the phoenix. The best of the scaled insects is the tortoise. The best of the scaled beasts is the dragon. The best of bare-bodied human beings is the sage." This quotation indicates, in the mind of ancient Chinese, all living beings including people were regarded as beasts and in the modern time, the tiger is still termed "大虫 (dàchóng: big beast)", the snake, "长虫 (cháng·chong: long beast)", the crawling beast, "爬虫 (páchóng: the reptiles)" and the rat, "老虫 (lǎochóng)".

In creating characters, ancient Chinese put three tiny insects together, to make "蟲", showing that insects used to get together. As a component of other characters, it is simplified to "虫" to make a balanced appearance, indicating various insects and it is used, for simplicity, along with the arthropod, the mollusc, as well as anything or acts having something to do with them as in "蚂蚁 (mǎyǐ: ants)", "蝴蝶 (húdié: butterflies)", "蜻蜓 (qīngtíng: dragonflies)".

qiū

秋

The ancient form of this character depicts an insect, indicating the time of year when the weather
turns cool and insects start appearing indoors. It was
later adopted to stand for the season of autumn, and eventually came to be written as "秋".

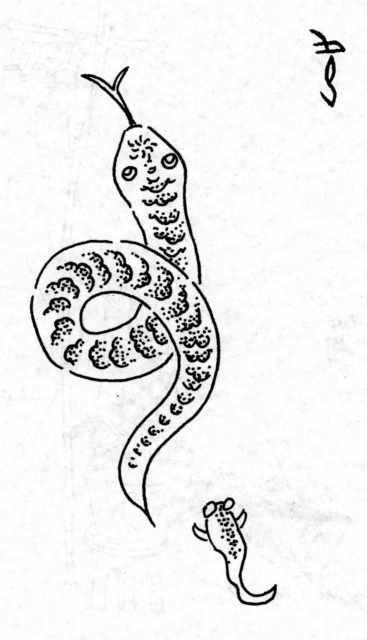

tā This character originally depicted a snake, which later
它 came to be represented by the addition of a "虫" to make
"蛇".

This character is later adopted as a non-personal pronoun.

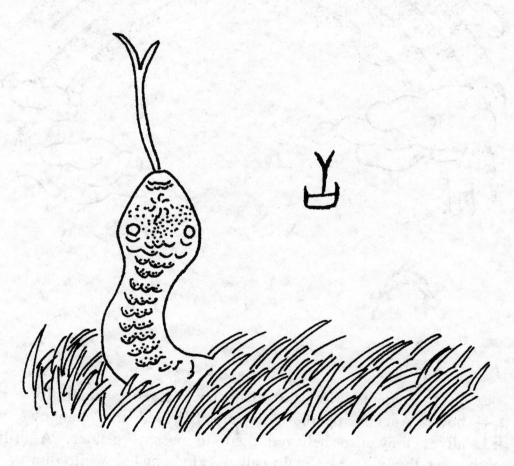

shé

舌 The ancient form of this character is a depiction of a snake's tongue, because forked out, the tongue is the most distinguishing characteristic of a snake.

hóng

虹

In ancient script, this character is a representation of a rainbow. Ancient people not only believed that rainbows were alive, they also believed them to possess gender. A brilliant rainbow was thought to be male called "虹(hóng)", while dim or secondary rainbows were considered female called "霓(ní)". "虫" is taken to represent the shape and "工(gōng)" is used to approximate the pronunciation.

yú
鱼   The ancient form of this character depicts fish, and is traditionally written as "魚". As a component of another character, it signifies something to do with fish.

gòu

構

The ancient form of this character depicts two fishes meeting together and means "to meet". Two people passing each other is termed "遘 (gòu : to encounter)"; an adult male and female becoming wife and husband is termed "婚媾 (hūngòu : marriage)"; a house built with timber is termed "構 (gòu : structure)" and simplified to "构"; a buyer acquires necessary articles from a seller with payment made in "贝 (bèi : shell)" and this is termed "購 (gòu : purchase)" and simplified to "购"; ancient people covered fires with cages and now people make fires with wood in fields termed "篝火 (gōuhuǒ : campfire)".

渔

yú　　This character depicts a fish in water, as in "打渔（dǎyú: to fish)".

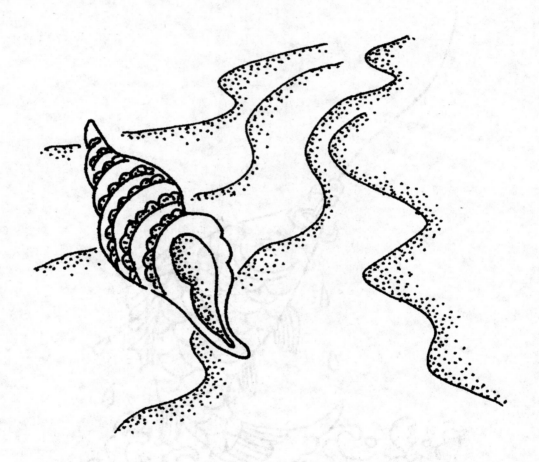

bèi

贝

This character originally depicted the form of a shell.

Ancient people used shells as money, and so as a component of another character, "贝" indicates something to do with trade or commerce.

The traditional form of this character is written as "貝".

jù

具

Inscriptions on shells and bone of this character depict two hands raising a cooking vessel (鼎), meaning "to make offerings". Holding something in hand means "具有(jùyǒu：to possess, or to have)" and "具" can also be construed as "工具(gōngjù：tools)" and "器具(qìjù：appliance or utensil)".

The character in inscriptions on ancient bronze is written as "貝(bèi：shell)" from "鼎(dǐng：vessel)", and in the style of calligraphy used on seals is written as "目" from "貝", and is standardized as "具".

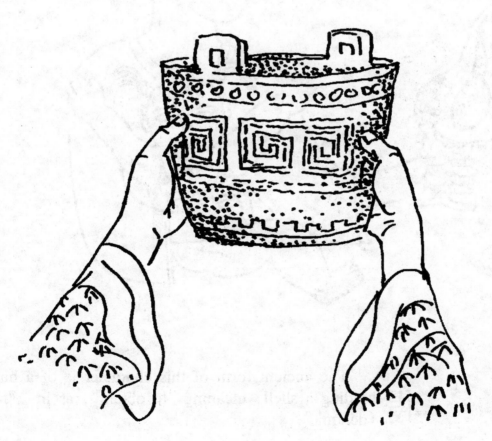

dé
得   The ancient form of this character is of a hand holding a shell, meaning "to obtain", as in "得到 (dédào)".

bài

败

This character originally depicted a right hand holding a stick and striking a shell. It appears in such words as "败坏(bàihuài)", meaning "to corrupt, to ruin". The traditional form of this character is written as "敗".

lóng
龙
The ancient form of this character depicts a great reptile, with hair on its head and a wide open mouth, representing a dragon—the magical creature form Chinese legends. Since ancient times, the dragon has been a symbol of auspiciousness, gratification, and power of Chinese nation.

This character is traditionally written as "龍".

guī
亀   Meaning "turtle", this character originally was
a sideview of a turtle. The traditional form of this
character is written as "龜".

cán

蚕

Meaning "silkworm", the ancient form of this character is a depiction of a silkworm.

The traditional form of this character is written as "蠶". In the simplified version, "虫 (chóng)" represents a small insect, and "天 (tiān)" indicates the pronunciation.

chán Meaning "cicada",
蝉 this character represents
such an insect in an-
cient script. Later, the standard
traditional form was written as
"蟬". In the simplified version,
"虫(chóng)" indicates a sort of
insect, and "单(dān)" provides
the approximate pronunciation.

gé   Take the skin off an animal, get rid of its hairs, and dry it

革 in the sun, and you have the original meaning of "革". In the ancient form of this character, the head, body, and tail of the animal can be seen at the top, middle, and bottom of the character. It can be found in the word "皮革 (pígé)", meaning "hide".

Leather is made only by going through several processes, and so "革" also means "改革 (gǎigé)", "reform".

皮 pí   The ancient form of this character depicts a right hand holding half of a " 革 (gé: animal hide)". It indicates folding up a finished hide. Thus, "皮" in ancient script refers to an action.

Later, "皮" came to mean "skin", or the outside or surface of something, as in "皮毛之论(pí máo zhī lùn: superficial opinions)".

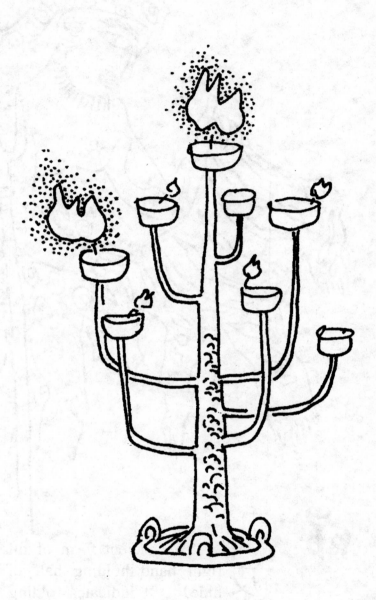

huǒ   This character originally depicted a raging flame, and
火 meant "fire". As a component of another character, this
character is written as " 火 " or " 灬 ", expressing something relating to burning, cooking, illumination, or heat.

yán

炎

This character is composed of two "火 (huǒ: fire)", meaning "very hot".

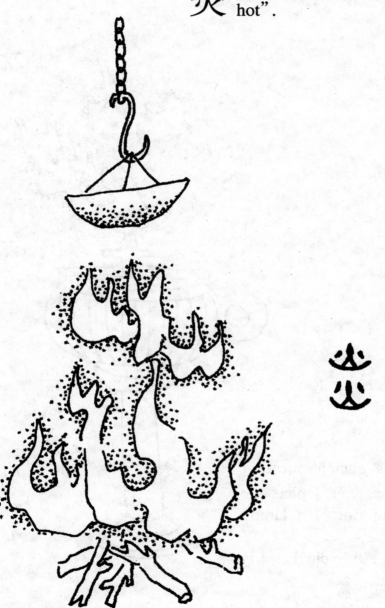

yàn The ancient form of
焱 this character depicts the
dancing fire of a lamp,
meaning "flame".

Eventually, this character is
standardized as "焱".

guāng
光　　The ancient form of this character depicts a flame held above a kneeling person's head, and means "光(light)" as in "光明(guāngmíng：bright)".

大
火

chì   In ancient script, this
赤   character is composed of "大
(dà: large)" and "火 (huǒ:
fire)", expressing the color of a
large fire. Thus, "赤" means "red".

312

fén
焚   People in ancient times would set fire to a section of
forest in order to trap boars. This character depicts a
burning forest. Thus "焚" means "to burn".

夕火

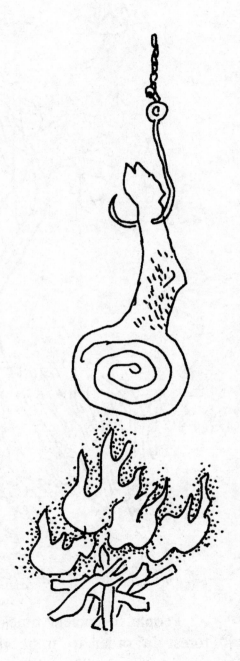

zhì

炙　The ancient form of this character depicts a chunk of roasting meat, and means "to broil, to roast". Because it is meat that is being roasted, this character can also mean "roast meat", as in "残羹冷炙（cán gēng lěng zhì: left-over soup and cold meat)".

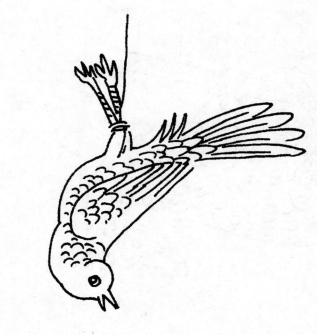

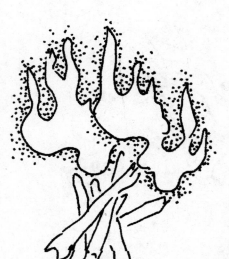

jiāo

焦   This character depicts a bird （隹）being roasted over a fire and means "to scorch, to burn".

In the modern form of this character, " 火 （huǒ: fire）" is written as " 灬 " to make "焦".

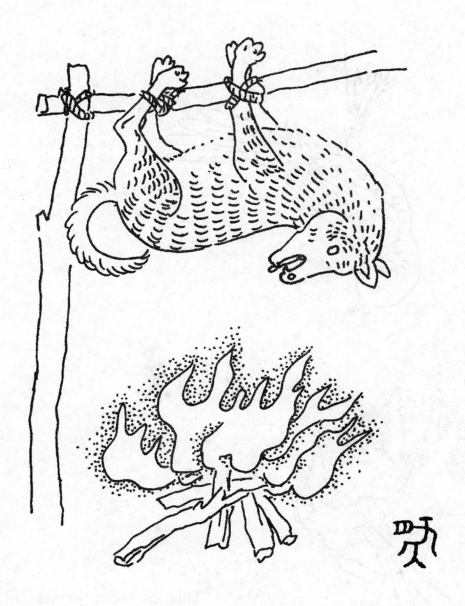

rán

然

This character depicts a dog being roasted over a fire. This is the original form of what is now written as "燃(rán)", meaning "to burn".

The character was later adopted as an auxiliary word, and a "火(huǒ:fire)" is added to make "燃(to burn)".

316

gāo
羔 The ancient form of this character depicts a sheep being roasted over a fire. Because the meat of young sheep is the most tender and delicious, "羔" later came to be used to mean "lamb".

SECTION THREE

HUMAN LIFE

shàng
上

The ancient form of this character is drawn with a short horizontal stroke on top and a long cursive horizontal stroke on the bottom. In ancient script, the short stroke on top represents something above; and so is the monarch by extending the meaning of the character. In spoken language, an emperor was termed "皇上". Sima Qian, in *Records of Historian, An Autobiographic Note of Tai Shi Gong*, wrote: "作《今上本纪》第十二 (write *The Basic Annals of* '今上 [*Jin Shang*]', Volume No. 12)." Here "今上 (Jin Shang)" refers to Liu Che, Emperor Hanwu at the time of Sima Qian. "上", signifying a direction, also gives birth to the meaning of "从低处往高处走 (to go up from a lower position)" and an example is found in a poem *Stand On Guanque Tower* written by Wang Zhihuan: "欲穷千里目，更上一层楼。 (Should you wish to get the distant view of the nature, You'd better go up a higher floor.)"

To distinguish it from "二 (èr: two)", the character is written as "上".

321

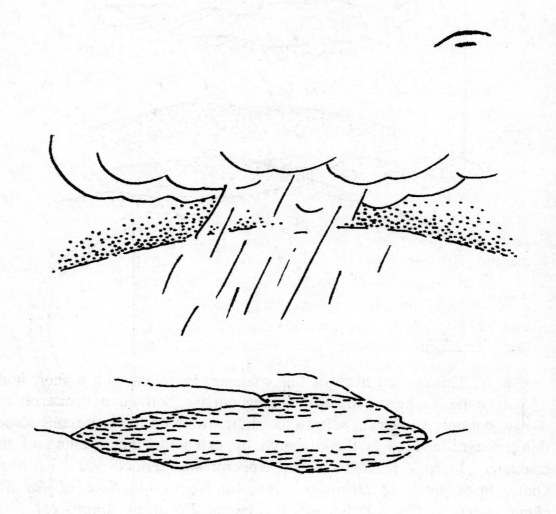

下   The character is written with a long cursive horizontal stroke on top and a short one on bottom, indicating something underneath and thus, originally means a direction, "beneath". Sima Qian, in *Records of Historian, Lian Po and Lin Xiangru Biographies*, wrote: "且相如素贱人,吾羞,不忍为之下。(Xiangru had been a mean man, so I feel humiliated and cannot be willing to rank next to him.)" Here, "下" means a lower position, an extended meaning of it.

322

gōng

弓 The ancient character resembles a bow, a sort of ancient weapon used as a launching device for arrows.

The grip of a bow is bent and curved, so this character also means to bend something, as in "弓腰曲背 (gōng yāo qū bèi)", meaning "to bend the back"; later "躬 (gōng)" means bending over, with "身 (shēn: the body)" indicating the general meaning, and "弓 (bow)" providing the pronunciation as well as signifying the meaning "to bend".

As a component of another character, "弓" usually appears on the left or bottom. In general, it signifies an object, action, or condition relating to a bow. For example, in the phrases "改弦更张,引而不发 (gǎi xián gēng zhāng, yǐn ér bù fā)", "剑拔弩张 (jiàn bá nǔ zhāng)", "弦" means "bowstring", "引" means "to stretch", "弩" means "crossbow", and "张" means "to draw (a bow)".

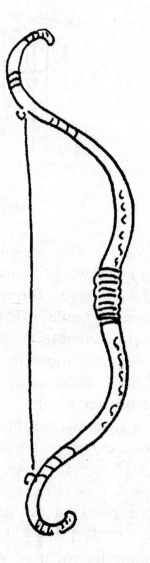

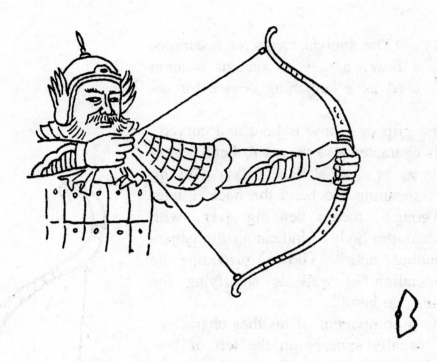

xián

弦 The ancient form of this character depicts a bow with a dot drawn to indicate the string. The idiom "箭在弦上(jiàn zài xián shàng)" illustrates the tension just before releasing an arrow or starting a battle. This phrase is used as an analogy for a situation that has developed to a critical stage.

A partial moon looks like a strung bow, giving rise to the expressions "上弦月(shàngxiányuè: first quarter moon)" and "下弦月(xiàxiányuè: last quarter moon)". Later, "弦" was also adopted to mean the strings on a musical instrument, as well as an arc in geometry—the line that connects two points on a circle. The great Tang Dynasty poet Bai Juyi, in his "琵琶行(*Song of a Pipa Player*)" wrote, "转轴拨弦三两声,未成曲调先有情(Pleasant rhythm has come to ears only by turning the peg while plucking the string twice or thrice, and temperament and interest are already presented before playing a melody)", expressing the artistic accomplishment of a woman *pipa* player. In this verse, "弦" refers to the string of the instrument.

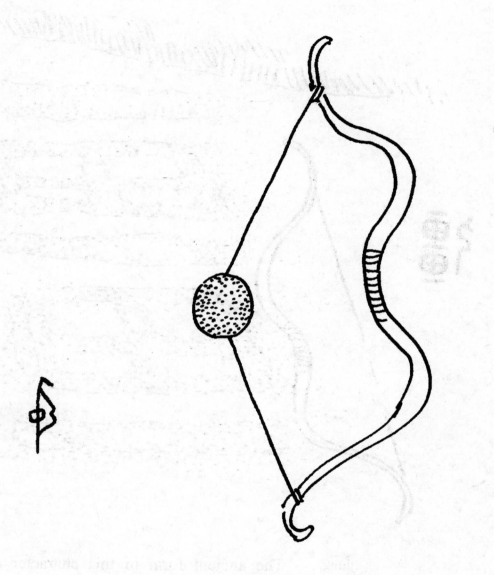

dàn
弹

The character is not self - explanatory. Ancient people added a "○" to "弓 (gōng: bow)", signifying a pellet. Later, "弹" was formed, with "弓 (bow)" indicating the meaning and "单 (dān)" providing the pronunciation.

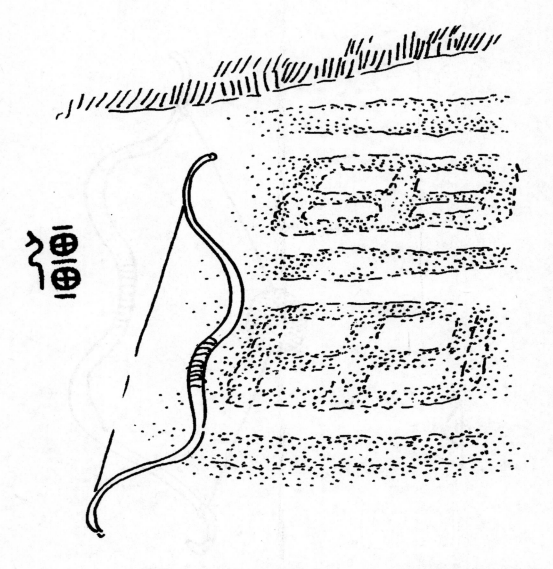

jiāng 疆 The ancient form of this character means to measure lands by a bow. Later, three horizontal strokes were added to signify the demarcation lines, and thus originally meant territory. The addition of "土 (tǔ: earth)" to "弓 (gōng: bow)" represents a later alteration.

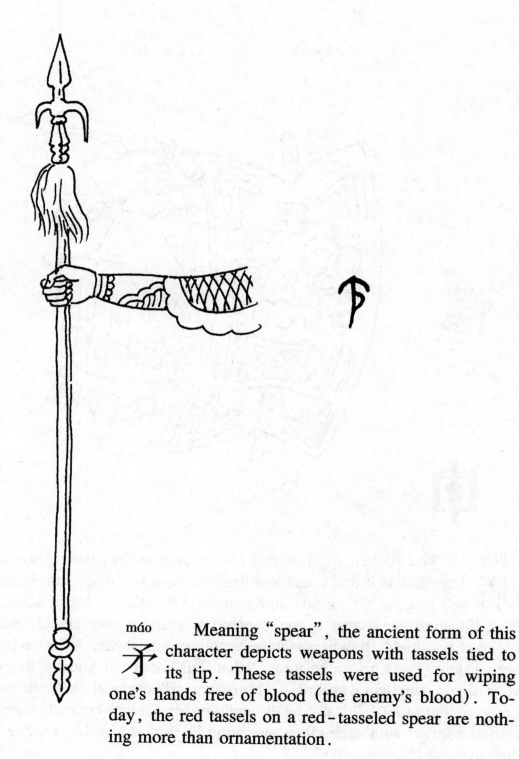

máo   Meaning "spear", the ancient form of this character depicts weapons with tassels tied to its tip. These tassels were used for wiping one's hands free of blood (the enemy's blood). To-day, the red tassels on a red‑tasseled spear are noth-ing more than ornamentation.

dùn

盾   The ancient form of this character is a depiction of a shield. Legend has it that in ancient times there was a man who wanted to sell a spear（矛：máo）and a shield（盾：dùn）. He spoke of how keen his spear was, that it was capable of piercing any shield; and he spoke of his shield, how it was solid as to turn any spear. A man who had been listening to him spoke up, "What will happen if you try to pierce your shield with your spear?" The owner could say nothing in reply. Later, people took "矛盾" as an analogy for when a person's words or actions conflict with each other, as in the idiom "自相矛盾（zì xiāng máo dùn：to contradict oneself）".

shǐ

矢

"矢" means "arrow". In ancient script, this character is drawn with head, shaft, and feathers of an arrow.

Arrows were an indispensable weapon in ancient times. The poet Qu Yuan in "国殇(*Martyr to the Country*)" portrayed a heroic scene in his line "矢交坠兮士争先。(Soldiers make advance, braving the falling crossing - arrows.)" Later, "矢" fell out of use by itself, but still retains its original meaning in such idioms as "众矢之的(zhòng shǐ zhī dì: the target for arrows or target of public criticism)" and "无的放矢(wú dì fàng shǐ: to shoot arrows aimlessly)". In these examples, "的" is pronounced "dì", and means "target" or "bullseye".

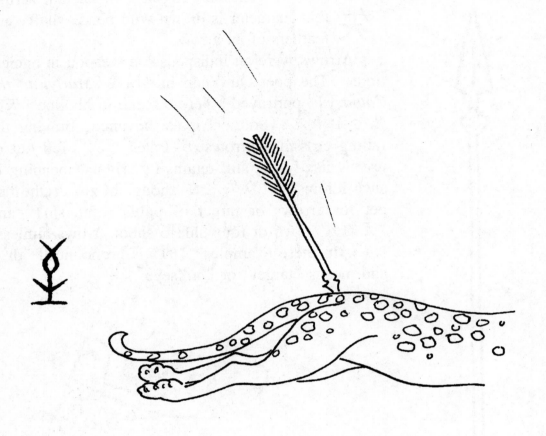

zhì

至 An arrow, when shot from far away, will stick in the ground vertically. Thus, in ancient script, "至" means "to arrive". The Tang Dynasty poet Du Fu wrote in his poem "石壕吏(*The Press-gang at Shihao Village*)": "一男附书至,二男新战死。(One of my sons sent word to me; The other two have died at battlefields.)" In addition, the idiom "宾至如归(bīn zhì rú guī: as if guests come back home, guests feel at home)". Both of these express the original meaning. Later this character was extended to mean a limit, extreme, or the most, as in "至尊(zhìzūn: the most respected)" and "至大(zhìdà: at the most)".

hán

函

The ancient form of this character depicts a quiver full of arrows.
Because letters are sent in special
bags, "函" is adopted to mean "letter", as
in "信函(xìnhán：letters)".

shè 射   This character, meaning "to shoot", depicts an arrow fitted to the string of a bow, ready to be let loose. Archery was an important aspect of ancient life, especially for nomadic peoples. Mao Zedong, in his poem *Snow* (*to the tune of Qin Yuan Chun*), wrote: "一代天骄，成吉思汗，只识弯弓射大雕。(And Genghis Khan, Proud Son of Heaven for a day, Know only shooting eagles, bow outstretched.)" These lines express the hunting lifestyle of the ancient Mongolians, and vividly embody the original meaning of "射".

Today the character is written as "射".

zhì

雉 A depiction of an arrow（矢：shǐ）being shot at a bird （隹：zhuī）, the original meaning of "雉" was "to kill" or "to injure". It was later used to mean "pheasant". The wife of Liu Bang, the first emperor of the Han Dynasty, was named "吕雉 (Lǚ Zhì)". In order to avoid the name of the empress, pheasants came to be called "野鸡(yějī：wild chicken)".

dòu

豆

The ancient form of this character is of a kind of jar or container filled with food. Probably in the Han Dynasty "豆" no longer referred to this kind of container.

dēng

登

In ancient script, this character appears as a "豆" with two hands and two feet. This indicates two hands elevating a ritual vessel filled with sacrificial objects being offered up. Because this character indicates something being presented in an upward direction, it came to mean to climb from a low place to a higher place, or "to ascend" as in "攀登(pāndēng)" and in the idiom "捷足先登(jié zú xiān dēng:the swift-footed first arrive)".

fēng

丰（豐）　　　"豆(dòu:container)" with two "玉(yù:jade)" inside, signifying to be full, means "丰盛(fēngshèng: sumptuous)", "丰富(fēngfù:plentiful)", as in the idiom "丰衣足食(fēng yī zú shí:to be well-fed and well-clothed)".

The traditional form of this character is written as "豐" and simplified to "丰", representing a substitute of the pre-Qin characters with the same pronunciation.

336

péng

彭   The ancient form of this character depicts sound emanating from a drum, and is an imitation of a drum being struck.

"彭" later came to be used mostly as a surname and in the names of countries and places. The addition of a "口", "嘭 (pēng)" indicates the original onomatopoetic meaning.

gǔ

鼓

This character depicts a hand striking a drum with a drum-stick, indicating an action. The saying "一鼓作气(yī gǔ zuò qì: to press on to the finish without letup)" has preserved this original meaning of "鼓". This character later developed into the noun "drum". Other words such as "耳鼓(ěrgǔ: eardrum)", "鼓着嘴 (gǔ·zhezuǐ: to pout)", and "鼓舞(gǔwǔ: to inspire)" are all extensions in meaning derived from the shape or function of a drum.

Today it is most often used as a noun, as in "敲锣打鼓(qiāo luó dǎ gǔ: to strike gong and drum)" and "金鼓齐鸣(jīn gǔ qí míng: All the gongs and drums are struck at the same time)".

^{xǐ}

喜

This character, composed of a drum (鼓) and a mouth (口), indicates a lively scene of laughter and drumming, and means "欢喜 (huānxǐ: happy)".

It is said that when Wang Anshi went to the capital to sit for the imperial examination, he was taken as son-in-law by a powerful and wealthy family for his outstanding talent and learning. As the popular saying goes: "洞房花烛夜, 金榜题名时。(On the wedding festivity of a man, his name appeared on the imperial proclamation.)" On this double happiness occasion, Wang Anshi wrote two large "囍 (double happiness)" and posted it on the door. Since then, "囍" has been passed down through the present day. When people marry, they will put up "囍" posters to play up the celebratory mood.

jiā

嘉

"嘉" was a very important component of rituals and propriety in ancient China. In the ancient form of this character, "口" expresses words of praise or blessing. The other components depicts a hand striking a drum, because bells and drums were absolutely essential in the course of spiritual rituals or hosting guests.

Later, "嘉" came to mean "happy" or "praise". The former meaning is expressed in a verse from Cao Cao's "观沧海 (*Viewing Vast Sea*)": "我有嘉宾,鼓瑟吹笙。(Zither and wind pipe are played in the presence of my guests.)" The latter meaning is expressed through such words as "嘉奖 (jiājiǎng)" and "嘉许 (jiāxǔ)", meaning "to commend" and "to praise".

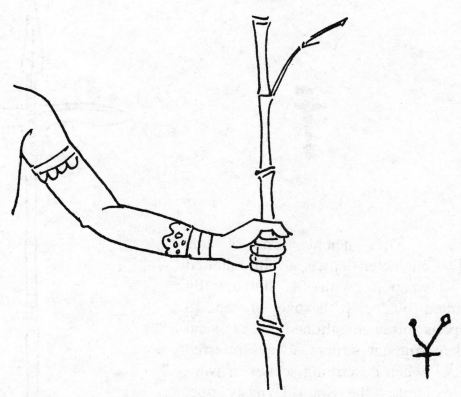

gān
干 The ancient form of this character shows a length of bamboo with a split end, which was an ancient hunting implement. Later this developed into a kind of defensive weapon. In the idioms "大动干戈(dà dòng gān gē: to go to war)" and "化干戈为玉帛(huà gān gē wéi yù bó: to turn swords into plough shares)", "干戈" refers to weapons of war. In a poem to the tune of *Po Zhen Zi* by Li Yu, "干戈" as in "几曾识干戈(What did I know of shields and spears?)" was borrowed to refer to war.

To take up arms is to eventually encroach against someone. This has led to the modern word "干犯(gānfàn: to violate)".

This character can also be pronounced "gàn", which is a simplification of the traditional character "幹". As such, it makes up the words "干活儿(gànhuór: to work)", and "干部(gànbù: cadre)", and has nothing to do with the original meaning of "干".

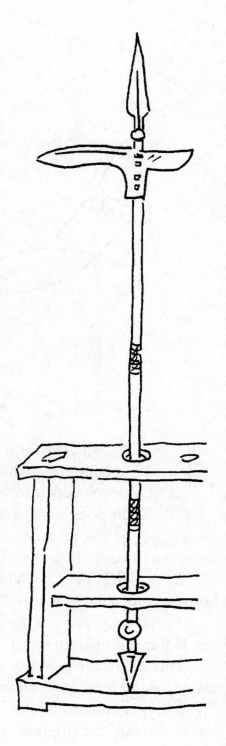

gē

戈 The ancient form of this character depicts a long‑shafted weapon with a horizontally mounted blade. It is one of the 18 weapons often mentioned in classical books. Ancient writers always referred to "戈" when describing scenes of war. For example, the Song Dynasty poet Xin Qiji, in his *Thinking of Ancient Heroes in Beigu Tower at Jingkou (to the tune of Yong Yu Le)*, wrote: "想当年，金戈铁马，气吞万里如虎。(In the years past, I, as a tiger full of vigor and militancy, Conquered mountains and rivers on horse with golden spear in hand.)" "戈" also appears in a number of words and idioms: "倒戈 (dǎogē: to switch sides in a war, turn traitor)", "挥戈 (huīgē: to brandish one's weapons)", and "反戈一击 (fǎn gē yī jī: to turn and strike against one's own side)".

shù

戍 Meaning "to defend, to garrison", this character depicts a man carrying a "戈". Today this meaning is found in the words "卫戍 (wèishù: garrison command)" and "戍边 (shùbiān: to garrison the border)".

jiè

戒 The ancient form of this character depicts two hands holding a "戈", and indicates vigilance, or "to be on guard against". "戒" in the idiom "戒骄戒躁(jiè jiāo jiè zào: to guard against arrogance and rashness)" carries just such a meaning.

伐

fá To use a "戈" to chop 伐 off someone's head, the o-riginal meaning of "伐" was "to behead". In the idiom "口诛笔伐(kǒu zhū bǐ fá)", "口 (mouth)" and "笔 (pen)" are tools, "诛″ and "伐" are syn-onyms meaning "to admonish, to censure".

"伐" can also be applied to trees, as in "砍伐(kǎnfá: to chop)". A poem from *The Book of Songs* reads: "坎坎伐檀兮。(Go to chop sandalwood.)" To go forth to meet a hostile force is "讨 伐(tǎofá:to suppress a rebellion or enemy)". Another line from *The Book of Songs, Dispatch Chari-ots* says: "薄伐西戎(bó fá xī róng: to conquer the forces in northwestern areas)".

345

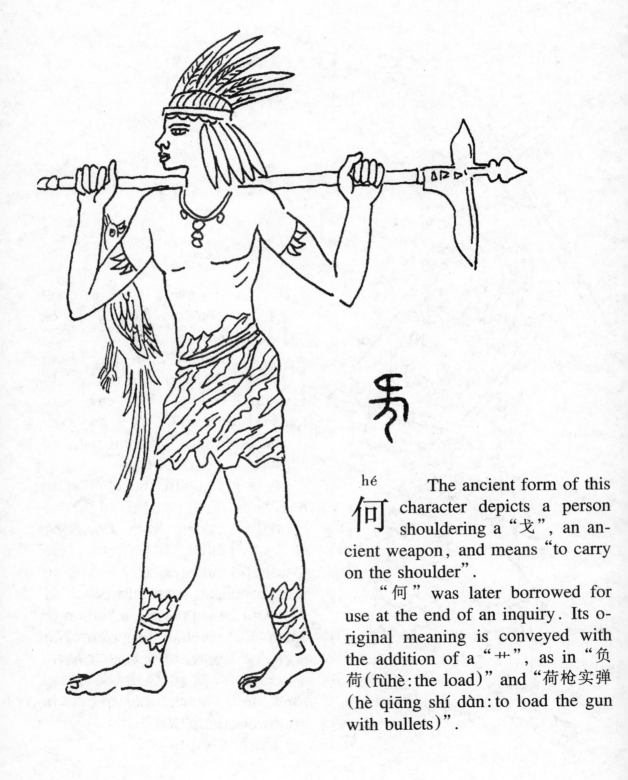

hé
何

The ancient form of this character depicts a person shouldering a "戈", an ancient weapon, and means "to carry on the shoulder".

"何" was later borrowed for use at the end of an inquiry. Its original meaning is conveyed with the addition of a "艹", as in "负荷(fùhè：the load)" and "荷枪实弹(hè qiāng shí dàn：to load the gun with bullets)".

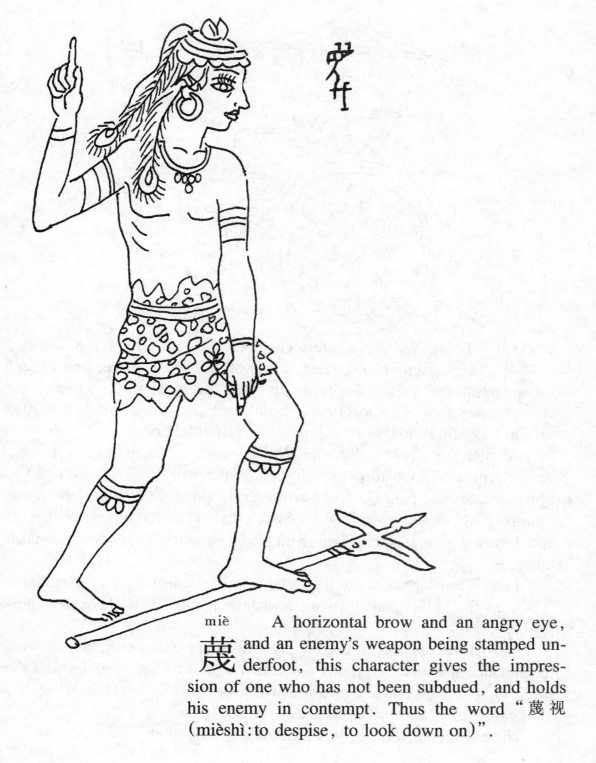

miè

蔑

A horizontal brow and an angry eye, and an enemy's weapon being stamped underfoot, this character gives the impression of one who has not been subdued, and holds his enemy in contempt. Thus the word "蔑视 (mièshì: to despise, to look down on)".

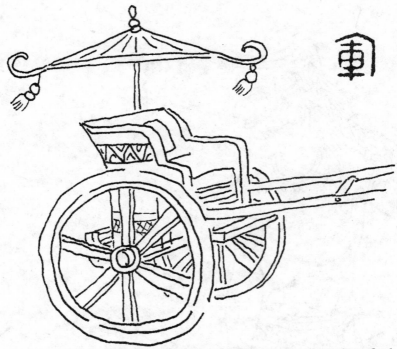

chē

车

In ancient script, this character is a sketch of the wheels, axle, carriage, and other details of a chariot. According to legend, the Yellow Emperor invented the chariot. Xi Zhong, the chariot master of Yu the Great, founder of the Xia Dynasty, is also said to have first thought of using horses to pull chariots.

Ancient chariots, aside from being used as daily transportation, were more used in battle, as reflected in the word "战车(zhànchē)". For example, the poet Qu Yuan wrote in his poem "国殇(*Martyr to the Country*)": "操吴戈兮披犀甲,车错毂兮短兵接。(Wielding our spears and wearing our armor, Fight with daggers when chariots cross each other.)"

Later, any apparatus utilizing a rotating wheel was also called a "车", as in "水车(shuǐchē: a waterwheel)", and "滑车(huáchē: a pulley)".

"车" often appears as a component in other characters, and is used to indicate all manner of items associated with wheeled vehicles and the like, such as "辆(liàng: a measure word for cars)", "轮(lún: wheel)", "轨(guǐ: rail)", and "辙(zhé: wheel rut)".

The traditional form of this character is written as "車".

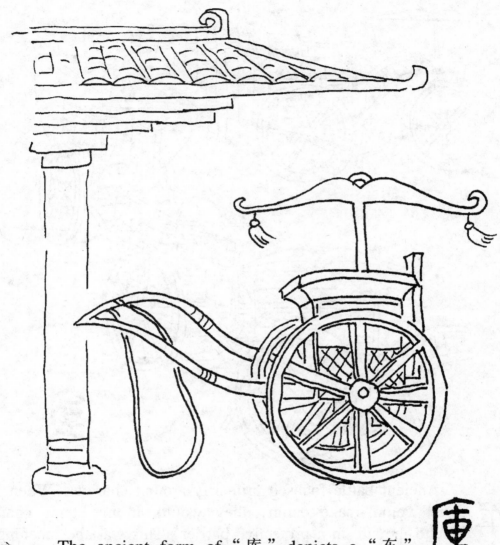

库

kù   The ancient form of "库" depicts a "车"
库 parked in a certain site, a place for sheltering
chariots, and means garage. Later, the meaning
of "库" was extended to mean buildings for the storage
of large amounts of goods, as in "仓库 (cāngkù: ware-
house)", and "水库 (shuǐkù: reservoir)".

The traditional form of this character is written "庫".

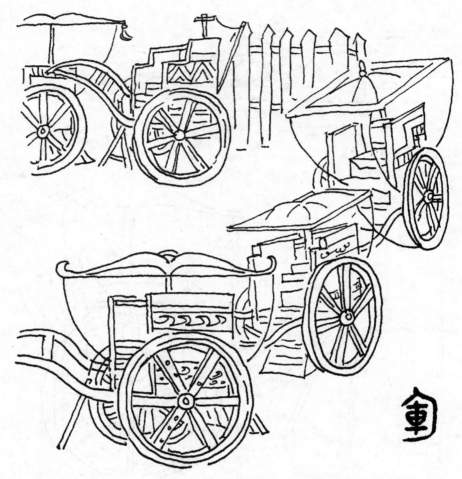

jūn

军

Ancient battle focused primarily around chariots. When soldiers would make camp, they would arrange their chariots around the site in a protective barrier. This was the meaning of the original character, which was a verb, meaning to garrison. In *Records of Historian*, it is written "沛公（刘邦）军霸上 (Pei Gong's [refers to Liu Bang, the founder of the Han Dynasty] troops stationed at Bashang [near present Xi'an and Xianyang in Shaanxi Province])", wherein "军" carries this meaning. The meaning of "军" was later extended to mean "军队 (jūnduì : army)".

The traditional form of this character is written as "軍".

zhōng   The ancient form of this character resembles and means
中 flag and with "口" drawn in the middle, indicates "中间
（zhōngjiān：the center）".

In distant ages past, various nationalities of Hua Xia（China）
lived in the Yellow River areas and considered themselves to be in
the center of the world. Thus, "中国（zhōngguó：China）" was
used to refer to themselves, while all other areas surrounding it
were referred to as "四方（sìfāng：the four directions）". Since
then, "中国（China）" has gradually come to be the special name
of the country.

lǚ

旅　　Originally meaning brigade, as in "军旅(jūnlǚ)", the ancient form of this character depicts two (or three) people under a flag, signifying people gathered under a military banner. In ancient times, 500 soldiers made up one "旅", and even today "旅" is still used as a unit of military organization.

Troops are most often stationed away from home, and so "旅" came to acquire the meaning found in "旅行(lǚxíng: to travel)", and "旅客 (lǚkè: traveler)". Another example is "旅居海外(lǚ jū hǎi wài)", meaning someone who lives in another country. The Song Dynasty poet Fan Zhongyan wrote in "岳阳楼记(*Records of Yueyang Tower*)": "商旅不行，樯倾楫摧。(Merchants and travelers were not to come, Masts collapsed and oars were broken.)"

xuán

旋　　Modern war is characterized by application of highly developed science and technology. Commanders are able to determine the victory a thousand kilometers away from the battlefields. The case was quite a different matter from ancient wars where flags used on the battlefields had great significance. The ancient form of the character is a combination of "𭅺 (flag)" and "止 (feet)", meaning soldiers moving around are subjected to the commanding flag.

　　"止 (足)" can also be written as "疋", resulting in the regular writing of "旋".

353

yóu

游
During the Shang Dynasty, the area controlled by the Shang was a cultural center. Many neighboring countries would send their young to Shang for education. The ancient form of "游" depicts a youngster holding a flag, meaning that he would be going to study in some other place or state. "游" later only retained the meaning of a person moving about, also developing into "saunter, stroll". The original meaning then had to be expressed with an additional character "学" as in the word "游学(yóuxué)". The original character was written as "斿", and later had a "辶" added to it to make "遊". This was later changed to "游".

zú

族

In ancient times, a group of people related through blood ties also consisted of a combat unit. They would each have their own flag to act as their standard in war. In this character, "方" represents a flag; together with a "矢 (shǐ: arrow)", "族" is formed, meaning a military unit. Later, "族" was no longer to mean a military unit but a clan, or any group of people with common characteristics, such as "家族 (jiāzú: family)", and "民族 (mínzú: ethnic group)".

dǐng

鼎

The ancient form of this character depicts a three‑legged cooking pot with handles. The largest "鼎 (tripod)" in the world is the "司母戊鼎 (sī mǔ wù dǐng: quadripod of the Shang Dynasty)", exhibited in China Museum of History.

Because a "鼎" is supported by three feet, three parts balanced against each other is called "鼎立 (dǐnglì: standing like the three legs tripod)". For example, the situation when the Chinese empire was divided among the three kingdoms of Wei, Shu, and Wu is known as "三国鼎立 (sān guó dǐng lì)".

zhēn

贞

This character originally was a simplified form of "鼎". Etching of laws on such ancient vessels was necessarily a very serious process, so "贞" means "firm, staunch" or (of a person) "to have integrity", as in the idiom "坚贞不屈 (jiān zhēn bù qū: to remain faithful and not subdued)". Ancient people often said: "贞女不更二夫。(A faithful woman will not remarry.)" In this case, "贞" was a moral concept used as a tool to oppress women in feudal society.

The traditional form of this character is written as "貞".

yuán

员

A circle written above an ancient vessel（鼎）represents the round mouth of the vessel and by extension the shape of a circle. Later, the "鼎" came to be written as "贝", and was placed inside a "口" to make "圆（yuán）", meaning "round".

From "圆", "员" meant "周围（zhōuwéi：around, surrounding）". In modern Chinese, "员" most often refers to personnel as in "人员（rényuán：personnel）" and "成员（chéngyuán：member）". The meaning of "around" is conveyed in the word "幅员（fúyuán）", which pertains to the area of a country.

The traditional form of this character is written as "員".

358

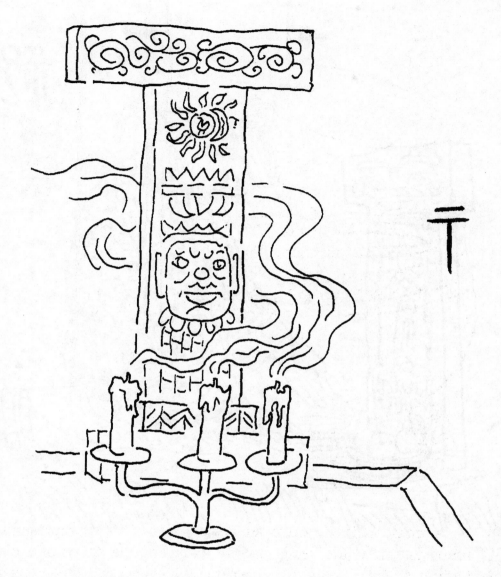

shì

示 The ancient form of this character depicts a tablet used in ancestor worship, and means "to show to someone". The Song Dynasty poet Lu You wrote a classic poem titled "示儿 (*Testment for My Son*)", which was written especially for his son to read, with the intent of giving him advice.

As a component of another character, it is often written as "礻", and is called "示补旁(shìbǔpáng)". It indicates something to do with praying, ritual, or deities.

sì   "示" or "礻" represents a memorial tablet for gods while "巳
祀 (sì)" represents a bending person. "示" and "巳" form the ancient character, indicating a kneeling person before the deities
and meaning "to pray". In ancient times, prayer was often related to
worship and so sacrificial rites constituted a significant part of life in
ancient societies.

lǐ

礼

"豆(dòu)" was a container used in memorial ceremonies and "玉(yù)" was an important sacrificial offering. The ancient form of this character, indicating two "玉" in the "豆", means to present to gods and pray for blessedness. From this meaning, various implications were derived such as "to express respect and politeness", "ceremony and propriety as well as courtesy".

In ancient societies, rites was the first of the six arts: "礼(lǐ:rites)", "乐(yuè:music)", "射(shè:archery)", "御(驭)(yù:charioteering)", "书(shū:reading)", and "数(shù:arithmetic)", and it was the most important subject for school education. "礼(rites)", as an indispensable part of China's civilization, not only covers all the social and moral norms in slavery and feudal societies, but also symbolizes China as a land of ceremony and propriety. "礼(rites)", as it was so framed in historical development, inevitably embodied such unreasonable and absurd norms as "三纲五常(sān gāng wǔ cháng:the three cardinal guides and the five constant virtues)".

To distinguish from "豐", the component "礻" was added to make "禮" and simplified to "礼", which was already in use at the time of *The Narration of Characters*.

qiě   This character originally symbolized ancestors by depicting a
且 tablet for ancestor worship. Because this involved the concept
    of rituals, a "衤(示)" was later added to make "祖(zǔ: ances-
tor)". Another interpretation is that this character depicts a kind of
table for placement of sacrificial meat during rituals.

"且" is now generally used as a function word.

yòng

用 The ancient form of this character resembles a barrel, and thus means "桶(tǒng: a barrel)". During worship in ancient times, offerings were often kept in a barrel ready for use, and "使用(shǐyòng: to use)" is derived by extending its original meaning.

jì

祭 The ancient form of this character depicts a right hand holding a piece of bloody meat, and means "to hold a ceremony" or "to offer sacrifices", as in "祭祀(jìsì)".

These rituals were an extremely important part of life in ancient China. Even during folk rituals today, people still place various food before an ancestral tablet. However, freshly slaughtered meat is no longer used.

祝 zhù   This character depicts a person kneeling in front of an ancestral tablet, praying to the spirits for good fortune. Today, it has lost any connection with praying, and is found instead in such words as "祝福 (zhùfú: blessing)", and "祝愿 (zhùyuàn: wish)".

365

dì

弟 The ancient form of this character depicts a person with a bow slung across his back. In the ancient past, when a person died, his body was placed outside a village and covered with firewood. To protect the corpse against hungry wild animals, his kin and friends would arm themselves with bows while transporting the body. Normally, if an elder passed away, his body would be delivered by younger people, such as a younger brother. Thus the character "弟" was created out of this ancient custom.

shū 叔 A character similar in construction to "弟 (dì)", "叔" is ranked third in the hierarchy of brothers (伯仲叔季：bó zhòng shū jì), meaning a younger brother.

"夫之弟为叔 (fū zhī dì wéi shū)", meaning "叔" in ancient times referred to the younger brother of one's husband. Today, one can still hear the word "小叔子 (xiǎoshū·zi)", which carries this meaning. However, "叔叔" is used to mean a man of one's father's generation, but younger than one's father.

diào

吊

This character is an image of a person carrying a bow who has gone to the outskirts of a village to pay homage to a relative who has passed away. In addition to "弟" and "叔", this character also represented the object of the ceremony, the deceased. Thus we have the words "凭吊 (píngdiào: to visit and ponder on the past)" and "吊唁 (diàoyàn: to condole)".

The proper form of this character is written as "吊", but sometimes appears in the non-standard form "弔".

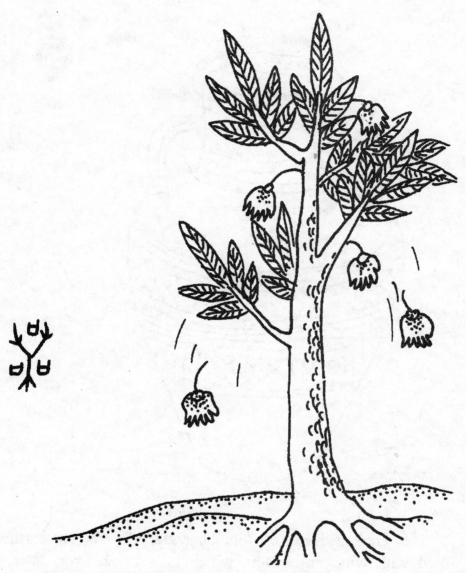

sāng

丧

"丧" means "death". Ancient people believed that falling blossoms were related to the death of people, so the ancient form of "丧" depicts unopened blossoms falling from a tree. Several thousand years later, in the classic novel *A Dream of Red Mansions*, the character Lin Daiyu sang in an elegy: "花落人亡两不知 (Who will care for the fallen blossom and buried lass)", which happens to correspond somewhat with its original meaning.

The traditional form of this character is written as "喪".

yǒu

酉

The ancient form of this character depicts an earthen vessel filled with wine, meaning "winejug". A "氵" was later added to make "酒 (jiǔ: wine)". Later, all characters having to do with wine, fermentation, and the like, had "酉" as a component.

Later, "酉" was also taken as one of the 12 earthly branches used in systems of dating and time-telling. The twelve earthly branches were used to denote the months, with "酉" being the eighth month. This indicates the time of year of ripening grain, which can be used to make spirits. As a unit of time, "酉" represents the period from seven to nine o'clock in the evening.

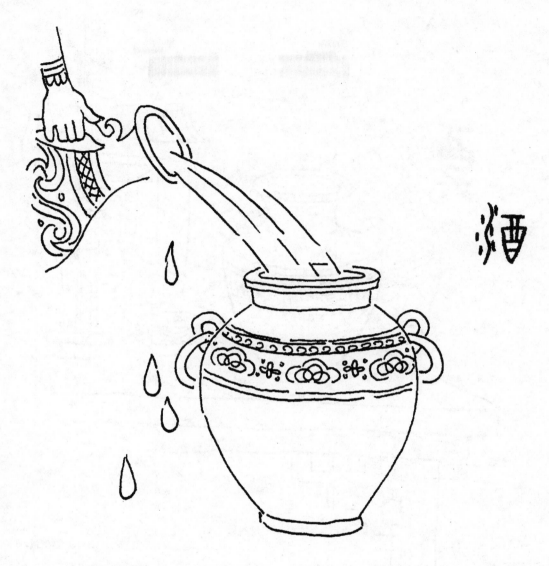

jiǔ

酒 　　Adding the radical "氵" to "酉" makes "酒", meaning "wine". According to legend, a man named Du Kang first invented wine. In a verse from Cao Cao's poem "短歌行 (*Sing While Drinking*)": "何以解忧，唯有杜康。(How can sorrow be allayed, Except Du Kang there is no other way.)" Here, "杜康 (Du Kang)" is used as a metaphor for "wine". People have since taken "杜康" as another word for "酒", out of recognition for Du Kang's contribution to Chinese cuisine.

diàn

奠 The ancient form of this character depicts a wine vessel set upon a ritual altar, an offering to deceased ancestors. It means "祭奠(jìdiàn：to hold a memorial ceremony)". Today, people often use a wreath of fresh or paper flowers to remember the deceased, so this character is no longer associated with wine.

jué

爵   This character originally represented a kind of three-legged wine vessel, and later came to be written as "爵".

Titles of nobility conferred by feudal monarchies are called "爵位 (juéwèi: peerage)". Today, the English monarchy still retains the system of conferring such titles.

zūn

尊 A depiction of two hands lifting a wine jug, "尊" represented a type of ceremonial vessel. Later, this character was adopted to stand for a different meaning of the same word, as in "尊卑(zūnbēi)", meaning "superiors and inferiors".

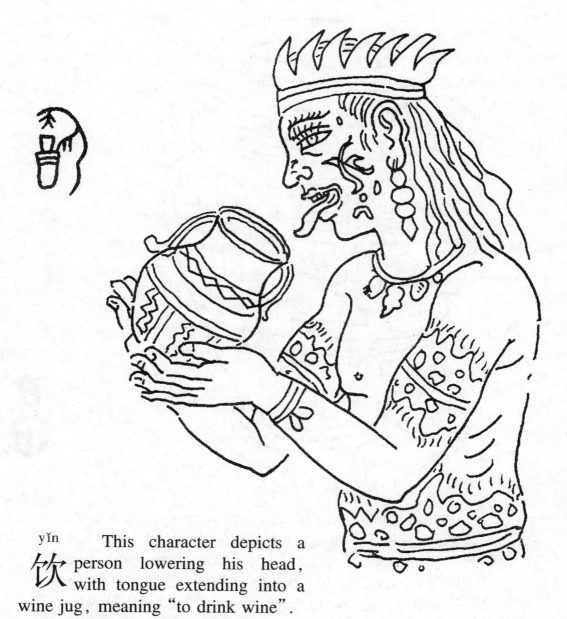

yǐn
饮
This character depicts a person lowering his head, with tongue extending into a wine jug, meaning "to drink wine".

This character evolved to "歙", then written as "飲", and was later simplified to "饮". Its meaning is no longer limited to drinking only wine.

bì

畐 The ancient form of this character depicts a wine vessel with a "十" in the middle, indicating "substantial". Later, many characters that incorporate some sense of "substantial" include the component "畐". Some examples are "福 (fú) ", which means to hope or pray (indicated by " 礻 ") for prosperity or well‑being; "富 (fù) " which means for one's household (indicated by " 宀 ") to have substantial holdings (to be rich); and " 逼 (bī) ", which uses the " 辶 " component, meaning "foot", to express "to force, to compel someone in tight corner".

fāng

The ancient form of this character resembles a container holding something, and another interpretation is of a container for the placement of ancestral tablets. Thus, the original meaning is a container holding objects.

"匚" by itself cannot be found in modern Chinese; and as a component, it still retains the original meaning as created as in the words "匣 (xiá:box)", "筐(kuāng:basket)" and "框(kuàng:frame)".

kuāng

匡

The ancient form of this character with sheep inside, signifies food vessel, and evolves into "匡", "王(wáng)" approximating the pronunciation.

The character is adopted to mean "匡正(kuāngzhèng：to correct)", "匡谬 (kuāngmiù: to correct error)" and then " 竹 " component is added to make "筐(kuāng)", indicating the original meaning.

378

mì

糸 The ancient form of this character depicts a bundle of wound silk.

This character most often appears as a component of another character, and can be found on the left, middle, or bottom of a character. It usually expresses something to do with fabric, printing, or dyeing. Written on the left or in the middle, it is known as "绞丝 (jiǎosī: wound thread component)". It has been simplified to "纟", appearing in such characters as "纺 (fǎng: to spin cotton into thread)", "织 (zhī: to weave)", and "辫 (biàn: to plait)".

^{sī} The ancient form of this character resembles two bundles of thread, meaning "silk". The sericulture in ancient China was extremely developed, producing a rich variety of silk goods. Therefore, the character "丝" came into existence from very early on.

For the ancients, the meanings of the characters "糸" and "丝" were one and the same. Later, a distinction is gradually made: "糸" is used more as a character component and is simplified to "纟", while "絲" is used as word in itself, later simplified to "丝".

sūn

孙   In ancient script, this character depicts a hand holding up a length of silk for others to see, indicating continuity. This character means "grandson".

Traditionally it is written as "孫".

jì

系　One hand grasping two bundles of silk expresses a connection between the two, and was the ancient word for "联系 (liánxì: connection)"."系" is also pronounced as "xì", as in "系统 (xìtǒng) or 体系 (tǐxì: system)".

jué

绝

A knife cutting a length of silk, the ancient form of "绝" means "to sever or to make a clean break". There are lines in *Dominator in Heaven* of "乐府(*Songs by the Music Conservatory of the Han Dynasty*)": "山无陵,江水为竭,冬雷震震夏雨雪,天地合,乃敢与君绝。(Mountains remain razed and rivers may be dried; In winter it may thunder and in summer it may rain or snow; The earth may come to one end of a line drawn by the sun and another star. How dare to make severance from you.)"

Because to cut off or sever also implies one has reached the end, "绝" can also mean "pinnacle" or "apex". The great Tang Dynasty poet Du Fu, in his "望岳(*Watching Mount Tai*)", wrote: "会当凌绝顶,一览众山小(Coming to the highest top, You will find all the mountains small)", wherein "绝" has such a meaning.

383

sǒ 索   The ancient form of this character uses a " 宀 (miǎn: inside a house)", a " 共 (gòng: two hands)", and a " 糸 (mì: silk or thread)" to depict a slave rolling fibers inside a room. Thus this character originally meant "to twist or wind", but can also mean "rope" as in the word "绳索 (shéngsuǒ)".

xiǎn
显   The ancient form of this character combines "日 (rì: the sun)", "丝 (sī: silk or thread)", and "页 (yè: a head)", meaning that under the bright rays of the sun, each strand in a bundle of thread can be seen clearly, as in "明显 (míngxiǎn)", meaning "obvious".

This character is traditionally written as "顯".

xī In ancient script, this character depicts a hand holding a rope 奚 that is tied around somebody's head, indicating a slave. Other people have interpreted this character as showing a person using one hand to steady a heavy bundle being carried on the head. Today, women in the Middle East and members of the Korean nationality in northeast China still practice this mode of transport. "奚" later came into use as a surname, originating with slaves.

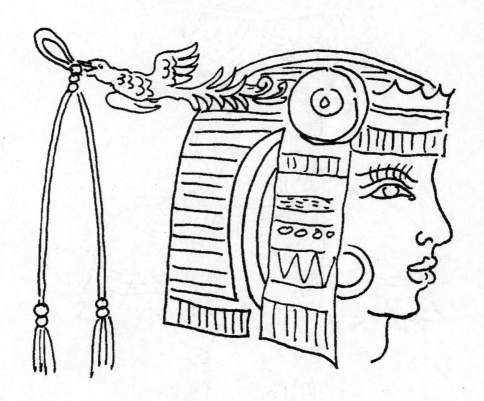

dōng   A knot tied in each end of a thread signifies
冬 "end" in ancient script. Icelocked winter signals the
     end of a year, so a " 仌 (ice)" is added below this
character to mean winter—the final season in a year.

zhōng   After "冬" was used to express the conclusion of a year, a
终   "糸(mì: silk)" was added to that character to express "终结
(zhōngjié: end)". For example, the well-known Tang Dynasty
poet Bai Juyi wrote in his poem "琵琶行(*Song of a Pipa Player*)":
"曲终收拨当心画,四弦一声如裂帛。(She made a central sweep when
the melody was ending, The four strings made one sound, as of silk
one is rending.)" Here, just this meaning is used.

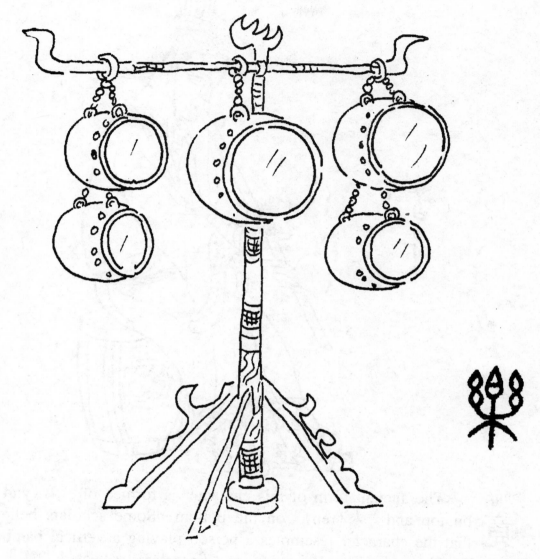

yuè
乐
      The ancient form of this character represents several small drums hung from a frame, meaning musical instruments of all kinds. In the history of musical development, the earliest musical instruments were probably percussion instruments, and the character "乐" reflects one of their early forms. "音乐 (yīnyuè)", meaning "music", is simply an extension of the original meaning of "乐".

      This character is traditionally written as "樂".

jìng

竟

The ancient form of this character is formed of "言(yán)" on top and "人(rén)" on the bottom. Some scholars believe that the character resembles a person playing a vertical bamboo flute. Xu Shen, in *The Narration of Characters*, selected "竟" as standard form, with top portion providing the pronunciation and bottom "人" as a variant form of a person, meaning end of a tone. An extended meaning is "to complete, or finish", as in the often-said phrase "未竟之业(wèi jìng zhī yè)" meaning something left undone. "竟" in the idiom "有志者事竟成(yǒu zhì zhě shì jìng chéng: Where there is a will, there is a way)" means "终于(zhōngyú: in the end)" and is a further extension.

jīn   This character was originally a depiction of a piece of cloth
巾   hung at the waist, later meaning "scarf". Rebel forces at the
end of the Eastern Han Dynasty wore yellow scarves on their
heads. In the poem "嘲鲁儒(*Mock the Scholars of the Lu State*)", the
poet Li Bai wrote: "足着远山履,首戴方山巾。(Wearing mountain shoes
on feet, And square scarves on head.)" The character "巾" refers to
this type of attire.

As a component of another character, "巾" appears on the left or
bottom, and indicates something to do with cloth or dress.

bó

帛

"白 (bái: white)" represents the color of rice while "巾 (jīn: scarf)" expresses a piece of undyed cloth. "白" also approximates the pronunciation of this character.

Before the Han Dynasty official Cai Lun developed the art of making paper, "帛", or silk fabrics, was the primary writing material, thus the words "帛书 (bóshū: books copied on silk)" and "帛画 (bóhuà: painting on silk)".

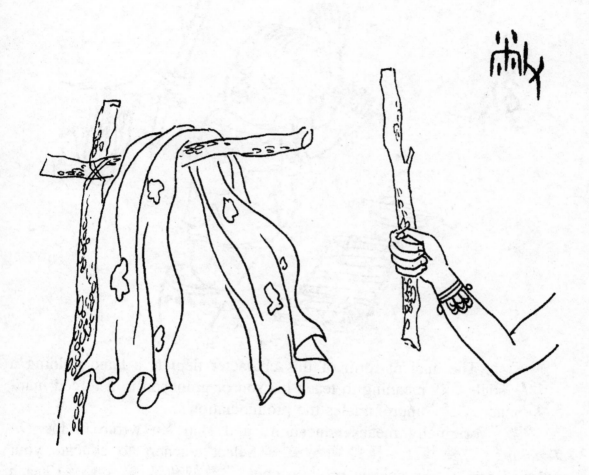

bì

敝 This character depicts a hole-ridden cloth on the left and a hand holding a stick on the right, indicating beating a cloth ragged. In the idiom "敝帚自珍(bì zhǒu zì zhēn: to value one's own trifles)", uses its extended meaning.

An old custom of the Chinese is the frequent use in a polite manner of the humble term "鄙人 (bǐrén)", which means one is ignorant and unlearned. However, many people mistakenly say "敝人 (bìrén)", which is quite erroneous.

jiào

教

The ancient form of this character depicts a hand holding a stick (攵) meaning to teach his son or grandson in a forced manner. "爻" approximates the pronunciation.

"教" originally means education, and Han Yu wrote in his *On Teaching*: "爱其子,择师而教之。(Select teachers to educate your beloved son.)" An ancient proverb goes: "教妇初来,教子婴孩(Teach the woman when she first comes; Educate the sons from childhood)", of which the first part means to teach a newly married woman how to abide by the female virtues, and provides an expression of the tie and control over women under the feudal ethics and morality; and the second part is self-explanatory.

The first great educator in China's history was Confucius, who made most significant impact on social virtues and ethics in the past two thousand years.

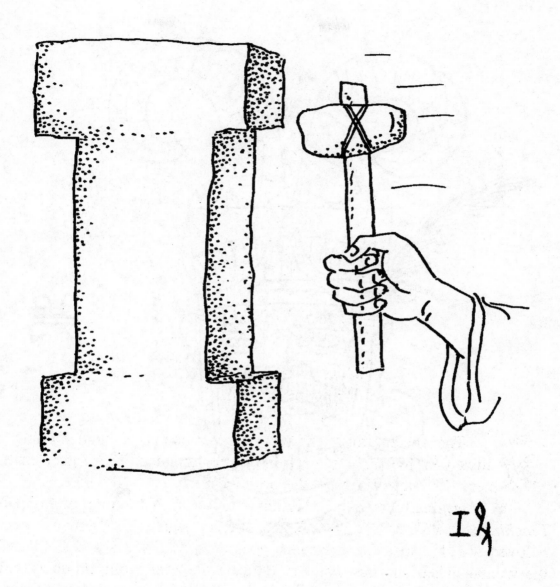

gōng

攻   The ancient form of this character depicts a hand with a hammer (攵), striking some object; "工 (gōng) " signifies an object of "H" shape and also is used to provide the pronunciation. The original meaning of the character is "to strike (敲击：qiāojī)".

mào

帽

This character originally depicted rams' horns used as decoration, often used by ancient southern tribes as head ornamentation. Even today, in Hunan Province the caps of babies and children are often embroidered with the heads of different animals, with two ears protruding from the top that are said to ward off evil.

"目（mù：eye）" and "巾（jīn：scarf）" were later added to express the characteristics of "hat".

miǎn

冕

Tradition holds that the Yellow Emperor invented the "冕", a kind of royal crown with jade tassels (called "旒", liú) hanging in the front and back. The number of tassels indicates rank. For example, the emperor's crown would have 12 tassels, while a prince's or duke's crown would have nine. Later, only the emperor was allowed to wear a "冕". A Tang poet, Wang Wei, wrote in his poem "和贾至舍人早朝大明宫之作(*In Reply to Jia Zhi's Poem Entitled Morning Court Session in Da Ming Palace*)": "九天阊阖(chānghè)开宫殿, 万国衣冠拜冕旒(The mythical gate to heaven is open to show the palaces, Envoys in various national costumes make obeisance to the crown)", describing the different dress styles of various foreign ambassadors paying homage to the Tang emperor. The idiom "冠冕堂皇(guān miǎn táng huáng)" meaning "stately crown" or literally "high-sounding", still retains the original meaning of "冕".

guān

冠

In the ancient form of this character, the "⋒" shape expresses a hat, while the rest of the character depicts a hand placing a hat on someone.

When the sons of ancient aristocrats reached the age of twenty, they would undergo a ceremony whereby they would wear a special hat, indicating that they had entered adulthood. This ceremony was called "冠礼 (guānlǐ)".

yī

衣   The top of the ancient form of this character resembles the collar, two sleeves, and front of an article of clothing, meaning a garment worn on the upper body. A line from a poem in *The Book of Songs* reads: "绿衣黄裳(lǜ yī huáng cháng:colorful clothes)", which conveys this meaning.

Later this character came to mean clothing in general, as in the prose "桃花源记(*Fabricated Story About the Peach Blossom Garden*)" by the Jin Dynasty poet Tao Qian: "其中往来种作,男女衣著,悉如外人。(People come and go from the farmlands, and men and women dressed really look like outsiders.)"

As a component of another character, "衣" is often written as "衤", which is called "衣补旁(yībǔpáng)". Written on the left of a character, this radical indicates something to do with clothing.

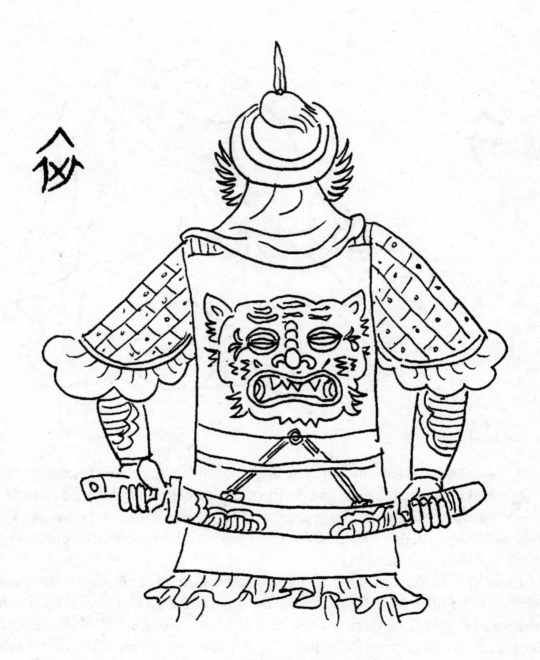

zú

卒　The ancient form of this character depicts a garment with a standard or a mark on it, meaning "soldier" as in "士卒(shìzú)" or "士兵(shìbīng)".

qiú
求
Showing clothing with hairs on it, the ancient form of "求" means "fur clothing". This character was later adopted to mean "寻求（xúnqiú）" or "探求（tànqiú）", both of which mean "to seek, to pursue". Other examples of this meaning can be found in the idioms "缘木求鱼（yuán mù qiú yú：to climb tree to catch fish）" and "刻舟求剑（kè zhōu qiú jiàn：to mark on the boat to locate the sunk sword）". Later, the component "衣（yī）", meaning "clothing", was added to this character to make "裘（qiú）", which holds the original meaning, as in the idiom "锦衣貂裘（jǐn yī diāo qiú：embroidered-silk and fur clothing）".

401

fú

市

"市" originally depicted a piece of cloth tied about the waist, but later evolved to refer to ornamentation showing the rank of aristocrats.

The earliest "市" was made of leather, and was written as "犮". Later, when silk became the main material, the component "纟" was added to make "绂 (fú)". As an ornamentation for officials, different colors expressed different posts and ranks. An example is given in the following verses by the Tang Dynasty poet Du Xunhe, in the poem "再经胡城县 (*Revisit to Hucheng County*)": "去岁曾经此县城,县民无口不冤声。今来县宰加朱绂,便是生灵血染成。(Last year by the county seat I passed, Elsewhere complaints were voiced from the common heart. Now the magistrate's ornamentation has been replaced by the red, That is dyed by the common blood.)"

zhǐ

旨

"勺 (sháo: spoon)" or written as "匕" on the top while "口 (kǒu: mouth)" with foodstuff inside on the bottom forms the ancient character, indicating "to place a spoon in the mouth", meaning delicious taste. *The Book of Songs, Section Xiao Ya, Yu Li* reads: "君子有酒, 旨且多。(Honest men have wine with different tastes.)" Later, "曰" took the place of "甘", and the character is written as "旨".

In the phrase "圣旨下 (shèngzhǐxià)", "旨" is borrowed to mean "意图 (yìtú: intention)", and "圣" refers to the emperor. Thus, "旨" as in "圣旨" specially refers to emperor's decree, and is not related to its original meaning.

mǐn   The ancient form of this character depicts a kind of vase or bowl with a base that is used as a container for food. As a component of another character, "Ⅲ", mostly appearing on bottom, can indicate all types of containers or related items.

xuè

In ancient rituals, the blood of sacrificial animals was drained into a container (皿: mǐn), so the character for "血 (blood)" depicts a ritual vessel full to the brim.

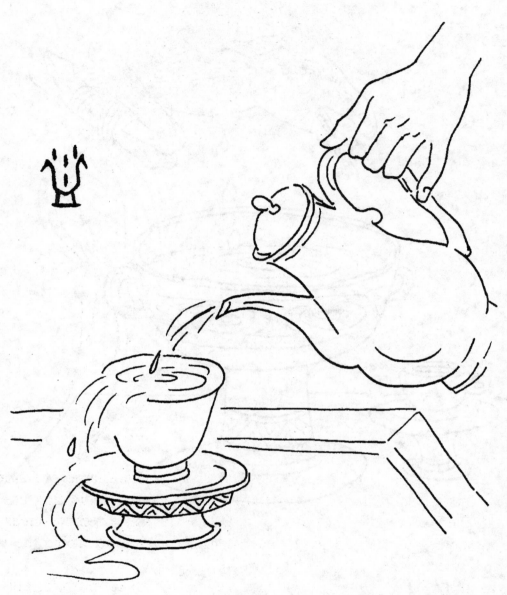

yì

益

In ancient script, this character depicts water spilling out of a container, and originally meant "溢 (yì: to overflow)". Later it acquired the meaning "增益 (zēngyì: to increase)", as in the idiom "延年益寿 (yán nián yì shòu: to prolong life)". Therefore, a "氵" was added to express the original meaning.

406

jiàn

监

The ancient form of this character depicts a large eye atop a body bending over a vessel filled with water, indicating use of the water as a mirror. Even today, in some remote areas of China, some women still have the custom of making up facing the water at a river's edge.

In the Shang Dynasty, people began to make mirrors out of bronze, and this character changed to "鉴(鑑)".

"人无于水监,当于民监。(Men may not look themselves in the mirror, but should draw lessons from the people.)" Here, the first "监" has the original meaning of using water as a mirror; the second "监", however, means "借鉴(jièjiàn:to take as an example)".

guàn
盥
Showing someone washing their two hands in a basin of water, this character means "to wash the hands or face". Today, restrooms in many places are called "盥洗室(guànxǐshì)".

jìn A depiction of a hand holding a brush, scrubbing out a con-
尽 tainer, this character originally meant "empty". Only when a
container is empty can it be cleaned, which is how this character
acquires the meaning of "ultimate". In the idiom "山穷水尽(shān qióng
shuǐ jìn: at the end of the rope)", "穷" and "尽" are synonymous,
meaning "end". In another idiom, "尽善尽美(jìn shàn jìn měi: being
perfect)", "尽" signifies attainment of some end.

The traditional form of this character is written as "盡".

鲁
lǔ

The ancient form of this character depicts a fish being placed in a container.

The fish was an indispensable part of ancient ceremonies. In *Strategies of the Warring States, Feng Xuan Visits Meng Chang Jun*, Feng Xuan sang while tapping the hilt of the sword: "长铗归来兮,食无鱼(The long hilt of the sword came back and no fish is served)", meaning he wished to be a distinguished guest attending an important ritual worship. Today, fish is still an indispensable dish for common people at festival feasts. "鱼(yú:fish)" and "余(surplus)" share the same pronunciation, signifying "年年有余(nián nián yǒu yú:some surplus left every year)".

The Lu State was the manor conferred by Zhou Gong who developed rites and produced music. He made the State of ceremony and propriety. The Shandong Province is the former manor of the Lu State of the Warring States Period, and is now still in short called "Lu".

410

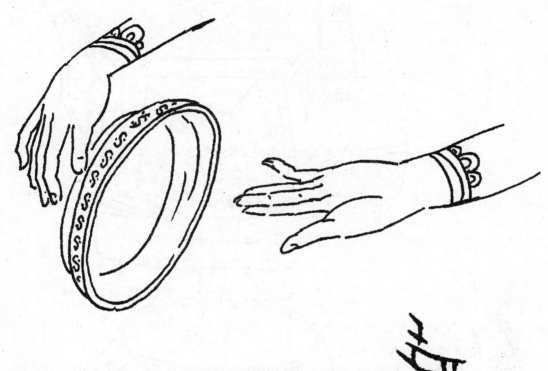

shòu

受

The ancient form of this character depicts a hand holding a plate and passing it to another hand, meaning "to receive". In ancient Chinese, "受" carries two meanings: "to give" indicated by the hand holding something, but with a later addition of the component "扌" to make "授"; and "to receive", indicated by the hand taking over something. Such an act is shown in "授受" appearing in the set phrase "授受不亲 (shòu shòu bù qīn)", meaning in giving or receiving, a man and a woman cannot touch each other.

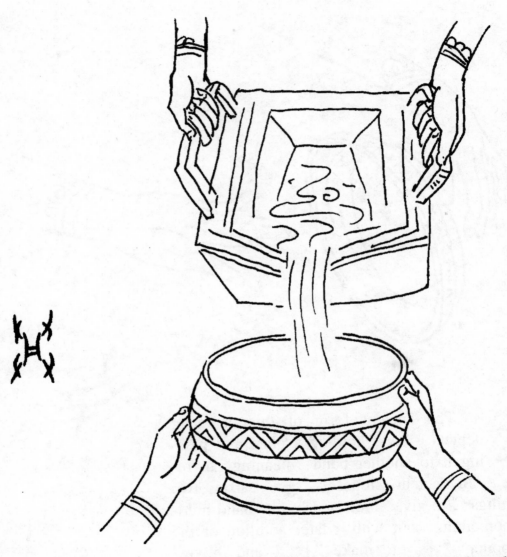

xīng The ancient form of this character depicts four hands
兴 lifting and pouring melted bronze into a mould, meaning
"to raise". Moulding and inscribing on it ancestral contri-
butions was a great pleasure and thus, the character, pronounced
"xìng", also carries the meaning of "高兴(gāoxìng:pleasure)".

yù

浴   In ancient script, this character depicts a person bathing in a large container, and thus, means "to bathe". In particular, in ancient Chinese "浴" referred only to washing the body while "沐" referred to washing one's hair. Today the combined use of the two characters "沐浴(mùyù)" means in general "to take a bath".

The traditional character is written as "浴" wherein the component "氵" indicates water while "谷" approximates the pronunciation. In ancient time, "谷" was pronounced "yù".

mò

沬 This character shows a person kneeling beside a vessel holding water. It means to wash the face and hair. That was the original meaning of the character. Later, it came to mean "泡沫(pàomò:foams)" and "唾沫(tuò·mo:spit)" as in the idiom "相濡以沫(xiāng rú yǐ mò:to render meager recourses to help when needed)".

lín

临 The ancient form of this character, depicting a person with wide open eyes looking down at an object from a high position, means "to look down" as in the idiom "居高临下 (jū gāo lín xià: to occupy a dominating position of height and observe downward)". From the meaning of "facing", the meaning of "imitation" is derived as in "临摹 (línmó: to copy)" and "临贴 (líntiè: to practise handwriting after model)".

yīn   The ancient form of this character resembles
因 and means plaited mat. Later, the character was
borrowed to mean "因为(yīn·wèi:because)" and
the component "艹" was added to make "茵", indicating
the original meaning, as in the idiom "绿草如茵(lǜ cǎo
rú yīn:Green grass looks like a mattress)".

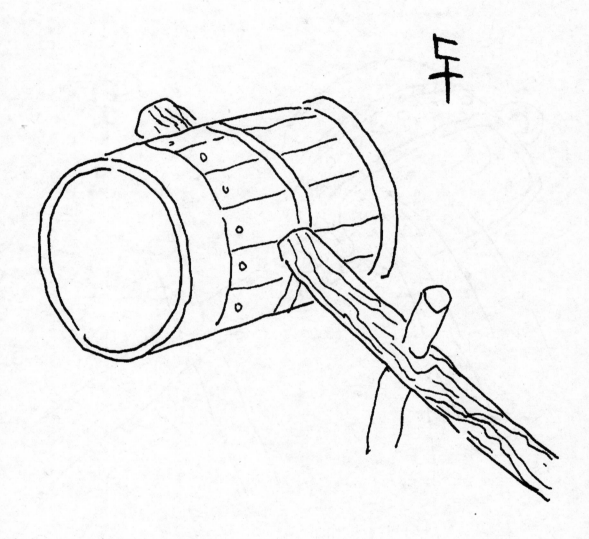

dǒu

斗 The ancient form of this character resembles a vessel with a long handle, and later, was used as a unit of measurement for weight as in the saying "海水不可斗量 （hǎi shuǐ bù kě dǒu liáng: Sea water cannot be measured with a bushel）".

417

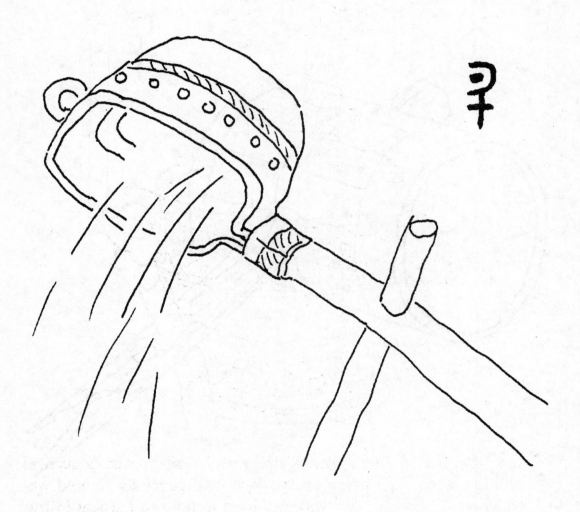

shēng Being also a vessel with a long handle, "升" is a smaller
升 unit of weight, accounting for one tenth of a "斗 (dǒu)". It
is added by a "一" to "斗" to distinguish between the two
vessels of the same type.

fǒu

缶

  "缶" was made in ancient times of various materials such as bronze, stone, and porcelain and was used generally to hold water or wine. Later, "缶" was also used to refer to musical instruments, as is recorded in "史记·廉颇蔺相如列传(*Records of Historian, Lian Po and Lin Xiangru Biographies*)": "秦王为赵王击缶。(Monarch of the Qin State struck '缶' for the Monarch of the Zhao State.)"

  "缶", used as a component of another character, most often appears on the left or on the bottom, indicating matters or objects having to do with a vessel.

hú

壶

Drawn with a big belly and a small mouth as a lid, the ancient form of this character resembles an ancient container holding wine. Today, it is called "酒壶（jiǔhú：wine vessel)". The traditional character is written as "壺".

420

huáng

皇

This character is formed with a base of an oil light. The light on top shines and so we get the meaning, "bright or brilliant".

Later, "皇" was adopted to refer to emperors in distant ages past such as the "三皇五帝(sān huáng wǔ dì: three emperors and five kings in legend)" to show respect for them. Zhuang Zhou in *Heavenly Fortune* says: "余语汝三皇五帝之治天下。(I say to you, three emperors and five kings rule the world.)" In the year of 221, Ying Zheng, Monarch of Qin State unified China and declared: "I am the first Emperor." Since then, emperor has been the special title of monarchies.

After the character was adopted to refer to the emperor or monarch, the component "火(huǒ: fire)" is added to it to make "煌(huáng)", indicating the original meaning.

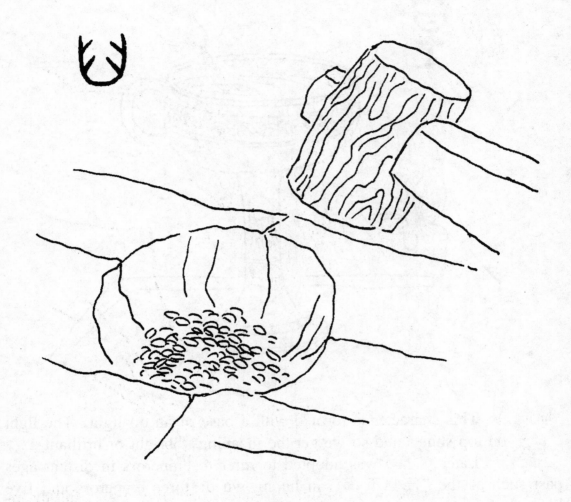

jiù   Ancient people dug the earth to make a "臼(mortar)". Later, stone mortar was used, for smashing rice or grains with a pestle, and the practice has lasted for a long historical period.

In ancient China, agriculture was well developed, and today "臼" or mortar, as an old production means, is still used in villages in remote borders of the country.

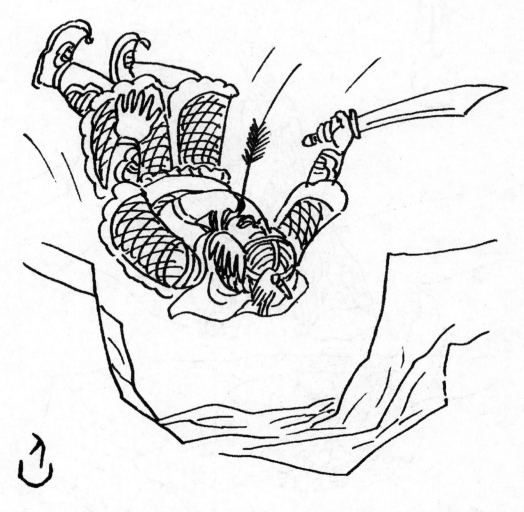

xiàn
陷

The ancient form of this character, depicting a man falling into a cave, means "掉入（diàorù：to fall into）", "陷落（xiànluò：to
be bogged down）". Later, a "阝(阜)" was added to make "陷",
indicating something to do with the ground surface.

From falling down into a pit is derived the meaning "to wrap up".
Thus, edible stuff made ready for wrapper（饣）is termed filling or stuff-
ing（馅：xiàn）, and enclosing them with fingers（扌）or splitting them
into parts is termed "掐", pronounced "qiā".

chōng

春 The ancient form of this character depicts a person standing by a "臼" or a mortar and smashing grains with a pestle in both hands. This long standing practice can still be found today in villages in remote borders of the country.

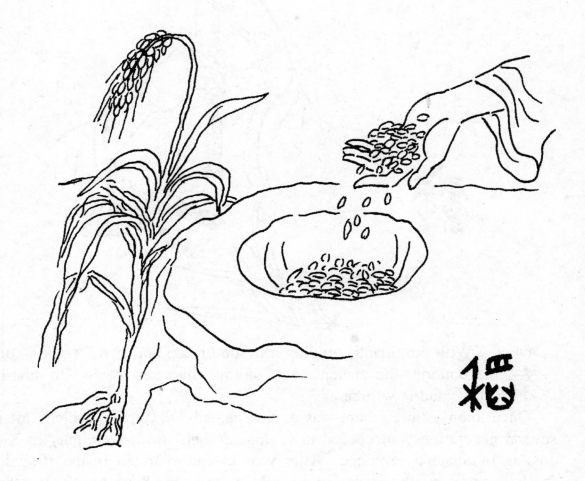

dào

稻

In ancient script, "稻" is formed of a hand (爪:zhuǎ) fetching rice from a mortar, and a "屮" signifying a flag or a standard used by envoy when paying tribute. This clearly shows that in the past, rice was already presented to the emperor as a tribute.

The traditional character is written as "稻" wherein "禾(hé)" represents the genera and "舀(yǎo)" represents the expression of grasping rice by hand and gives it its pronunciation.

qín

秦

With both hands holding a pestle on top and two "禾(hé)" on the bottom, the ancient form of this character means "to smash grain" and is written as "秦".

Once upon a time, there was a tribe named "秦(qín)", which, after several generations, succeeded in setting up their own sovereignty in Xianyang of Shaanxi Province. After year in and year out in the struggle for hegemony by the various monarchies, the Qin State terminated the other six powers. "六王毕,四海一(After the fall of the six states, China was unified)", and the first feudal dynasty in China's history was born.

Xianyang and the surrounding areas had fertile soil where developed irrigation was established and grain crops were grown. Because these areas were the manor of the Qin State in the Spring and Autumn Period and the Warring States Period, it acquired the good name "八百里秦川 (bā bǎi lǐ qín chuān: eight hundred li of Qin land)", referring to areas of today's Shaanxi and Gansu provinces.

426

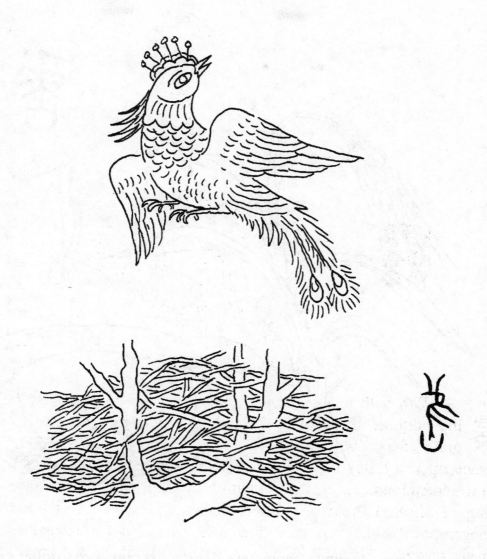

jiù

旧   The ancient form of this character depicts a bird flying out from a "巢(cháo：nest)". Some people hold that "臼(jiù)" provides the pronunciation. Later, "臼", originally a bird's name, is adopted to mean "旧(old or used)" as in "新旧(xīnjiù：new and old)".

The traditional character is written as "舊".

427

xiāng

香   This ancient character depicts broomcorn millet and wheat in a vessel emitting fragrance. The Tang Dynasty poet Pi Rixiu wrote in his "橡媼叹 (*Complaint of a Nutting Old Woman*)": "山前有熟稻,紫穗袭人香 (Rice before the mountain is ripe, People are assailed by the fragrance from the spike)", wherein the original meaning is used. Later, "香" is used in a general sense, referring to a pleasant smell.

hé

合

In ancient script, this character signifies a cover is being put on a vessel, meaning "相合(xiānghé: to coincide)". Followers and pious believers of Buddhism, when worshiping the Buddha, put their palms together, or in Chinese "双手合十(shuāng shǒu hé shí)". Another example is found in the idiom "天作之合(tiān zuò zhī hé: marriage arranged by god)" wherein meaning of the character is extended to "匹配(pǐpèi: to match each other)", "配合(pèihé: to be harmoniously combined)".

Ancient Chinese termed a battle as one round, and an example can be found in "史记·萧相国世家(*Records of Historian*, *Aristocratic Family of Prime Minister Xiao He*)": "多者百余战,少者数十合。(At most a hundred battles, or at least several tens of rounds.)" Since then the meaning has been in use and is found in the classic novels such as *Outlaws of the Marsh*, *Romans of the Three Kingdoms*, etc.

429

huì

会 With a cover on top, a vessel on the bottom and a pile of grain in the middle holding it together, the ancient form of this character means "会合 (huìhé: to meet together)", "聚会 (jùhuì: to gather)", as in the idiom "适逢其会 (shì féng qí huì: to happen to be present at the right moment)" and in the lines from a poem titled "燕歌行 (*Thinking of My Husband Who Is Far Away*)" written by Cao Pi, "别日何易会日难，山川悠远路漫漫。(It is more difficult to meet on some day than to part on this day, The roads to cover are long and mountains and rivers lie far away.)"

Associative compounds are the means to create Chinese characters, or one of the six categories of Chinese characters, which, by combining the meaning of each of the components into one character, creates another meaning. An example is that a person (人 or 亻: rén) leaning against a tree (木: mù) to make "休" as in "休息 (xiū·xi: rest)".

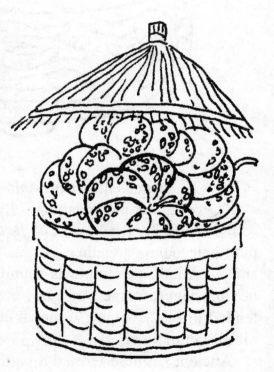

shí

食 The form of this character depicts a doorway of a granary on top and a vessel with rice inside it on the bottom. Because it is a granary, the character carries the meaning "to eat", which can be found in *The Book of Songs*: "硕鼠硕鼠，无食我黍。(Large mice, Large mice, do not eat my rice.)" According to Mencius, "民以食为天 (People regard food as sacred as god)", which has guided the development in agriculture for several thousand years in China. From "being eaten", "缺损 (quēsǔn: shortage or loss)" is derived, and so a solar eclipse appearing on the first day of a month on a lunar calendar is termed as "日蚀 (rìshí)" or "日食 (rìshí)" while a lunar eclipse appearing approximately on the 15th day of a month is termed as "月蚀 (yuèshí)" or "月食 (yuèshí)".

"食", when used as component of another character, is written on the left and simplified to "饣", indicating objects having to do with food.

jí

即

Depicting a person sitting before a vessel holding food, the ancient form of this character means "就餐(jiùcān：to sit at dinner table)", "就位(jiùwèi：to be seated)".

From the above meaning, the character also takes on the meaning of "靠近(kàojìn：close to)", as in the idiom "若即若离(ruò jí ruò lí：to be neither close nor distant)", "可望而不可即(kě wàng ér bù kě jí：No access can be made to something though in sight)".

In feudal society, emperors coming in power was termed "即位", wherein "即" means "to come to".

jì

既
Having a bellyful and turning the head to look round, the ancient form of the character means "已经(yǐjīng: already)" and the original meaning can be found in "既成事实(jì chéng shì shí: accomplished facts)", "既往不咎(jì wǎng bù jiù: to forgive one's misdeeds done in the past)" and "一言既出，驷马难追(yī yán jì chū, sì mǎ nán zhuī: A word, once said, cannot be captured even by speedy horses)".

xiāng

乡   The ancient form of this character depicts two people facing each other by a vessel with food inside it, and means "to dine (飨: xiǎng)". In the Zhou Dynasty, "乡" was an administrative unit with 12,500 households, and today is an administrative unit under the county level.

The traditional character is written as "鄉".

chuáng

疒

The ancient form of this character depicts a person lying in bed, meaning "to be ill (生病：shēngbìng)". The component "疒" is termed "病字头(bìngzìtóu：component indicating disease)", indicating objects having to do with disease.

mèng

梦　　With a man lying in bed with wide open eyes, the ancient form of this character signifies looking at something while sleeping and means "做梦（zuòmèng：to dream）".

The ancient character is written as " 寢 ", and later written as "夢". It has been simplified to "梦" since the Song and Yuan dynasties.

jí

疾

The ancient form of this character indicates someone who has been wounded by an arrow, a type of ancient weapon. In ancient times, "疾" and "病(bìng)" differed; ordinary diseases were termed "疾", while serious illness was termed "病". Today, both words used together refer to various diseases in general.

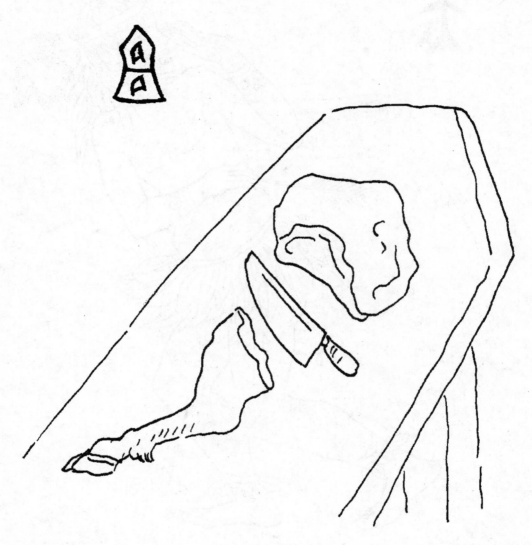

zǔ

俎

With meat on a table（且）, the ancient form of this character signifies an implement on which to display the offerings as the meat of animals during worshiping ceremonies. Later, the character was used to refer to a chopping board. Sima Qian said in "史记·项羽本记（*Records of Historian, Basic Annals of Xiang Yu*）": "人为刀俎，我为鱼肉。(Others are compared to knives and chopping board while I am compared to fish and meat.)"

438

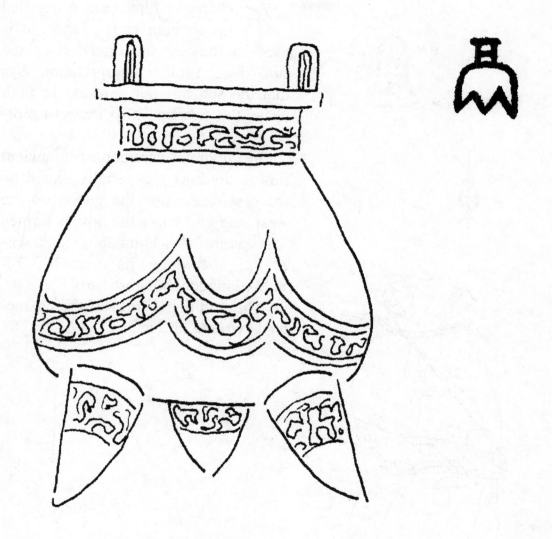

lì
鬲
The ancient form of this character represents an ancient cooking vessel with a big belly and three legs. The characteristic distinguishing it from "鼎 (dǐng: also a cooking vessel)" is the three empty legs which, with water inside it, can increase the surface area receiving heat from fire.

The character can be used as a component, as in "融" appearing in "春意融融(chūn yì róng róng: Spring turns the air warm)".

dōng

东

In ancient script, this character represents a bag tied up on both ends. Later, it is used to indicate the direction of the sun-rise. Another interpretation says that the sun has not gone up as high up as the tree tip, also indicating direction.

In important ceremonies in ancient times, the host was usually seated on the east side while the guests on the west side and thus, the host is termed "东" as in "房东(fángdōng:landowner)", "东家(dōng·jia:owner)", "东道主(dōngdàozhǔ:host party)".

The traditional form of the character is written as "東".

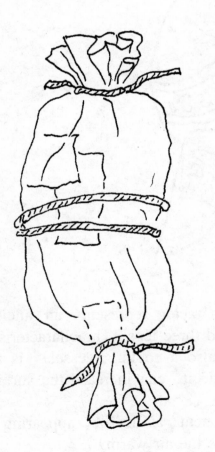

lù

录

With a well sweep atop and a container with drops of water beside it on the bottom, the ancient form of this character signifies a windlass for raising water from a well.

The character was adopted to mean "记载（jìzǎi：to record）", "抄写（chāoxiě：to copy）". In ancient times, a knife could be used as a pen. Knives could be used to inscribe on bronze vessels important events having to do with worship, military expeditions, weather and farming activities. Therefore, the traditional character is written as "錄" with a "金（metal）" as a side component.

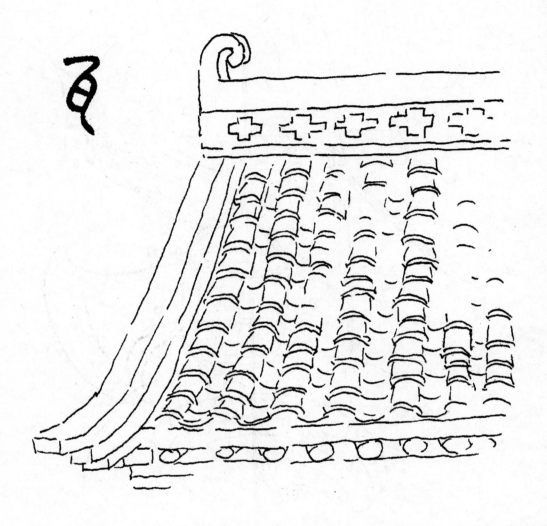

wǎ　　The form of this character represents tiles atop a house. The
瓦　character cannot be found in the inscriptions on bone and shell
nor in the inscriptions on any bronze objects, because tiles had
not come into existence until the Han Dynasty, as we usually say "秦
砖汉瓦(qín zhuān hàn wǎ: bricks of the Qin Dynasty and tiles of the
Han Dynasty)". In the Eastern Han Dynasty, tiles became a general
term for all ready-made porcelain products.

"瓦" as a component often appears on the bottom or right side of
another character, indicating objects having to do with porcelain.

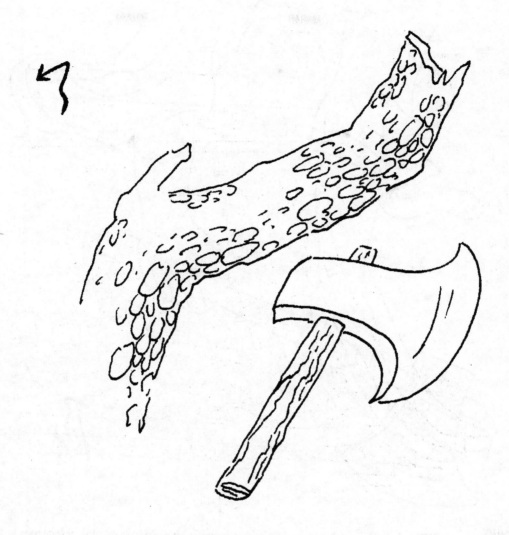

jīn

斤　　In ancient Chinese, "斤" represented an axe with a short handle. A small bronze axe with an arc edge, made in the Shang Dynasty and unearthed in 1954 in Ningxiang, Hunan Province, was named "斤". "斤" as a component appears on the right side or bottom of another character, indicating tools or action having to do with cutting, as in "斧(fǔ:axe)", "斩(zhǎn:to chop)", "断(duàn:to break)".

　　Later, "斤" is adopted as a unit of weight, as in "斤(*jin* = 1/2 kilogram)两(*liang* = 50 grams)".

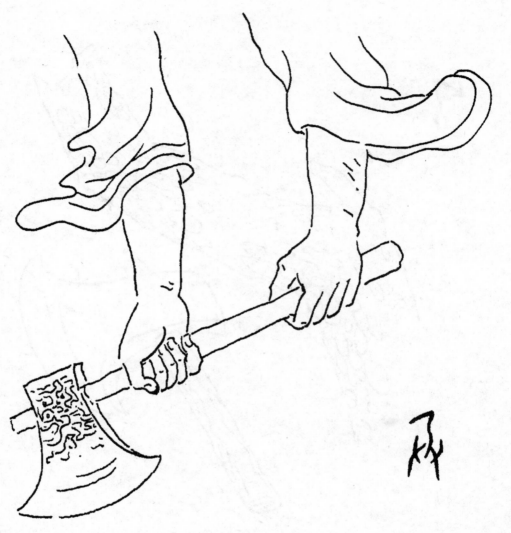

bīng

兵 With a "斤 (jīn)" atop and two hands on the bottom, this ancient character depicts two hands holding an axe, and means "兵器 (bīngqì: weapon)". The meaning is found in the idioms "短兵相接 (duǎn bīng xiāng jiē: to fight at close quarters)", "秣马厉兵 (mò mǎ lì bīng: to get the horses fed and weapons sharpened)", "兵不血刃 (bīng bù xuè rèn: The weapons are not stained with blood)". Later, the meaning extends to refer to "soldiers", "military", as in "士兵 (shìbīng: soldier)", "兵法 (bīngfǎ: art of war)", "纸上谈兵 (zhǐ shàng tán bīng: to keep practising the use of arms only on paper)".

444

fǔ

斧 This ancient character resembles an axe and is written as "斧", wherein "父（fù）" represents the meaning classification and the pronunciation while "斤（jīn）" represents the scope of the meaning.

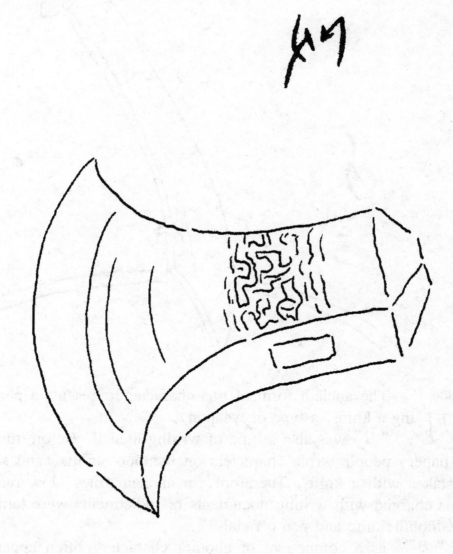

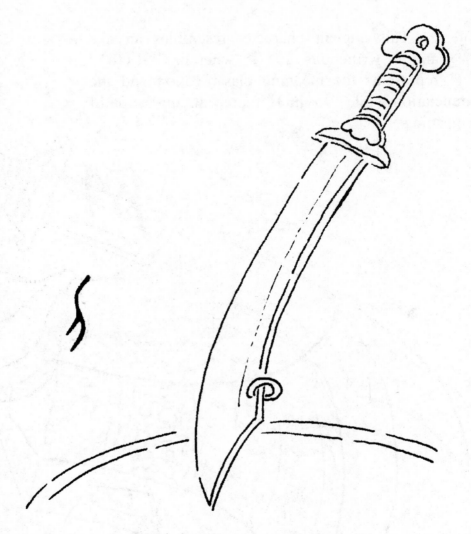

dāo

刀

The ancient form of this character represents a person carrying a knife, a type of weapon.

"刀" was also a type of writing utensil. Before the invention of paper, people wrote characters on bamboo scrolls, and scraped off mistakes with a knife. Therefore, in ancient times, low ranking officials charged with writing documents or indictments were termed "刀笔吏（dāobǐlì：knife and pen officials）".

"刀", as a component of another character, often appears on the bottom or, when written as "刂" （named standing knife component） on right side, indicates objects having to do with cutting.

446

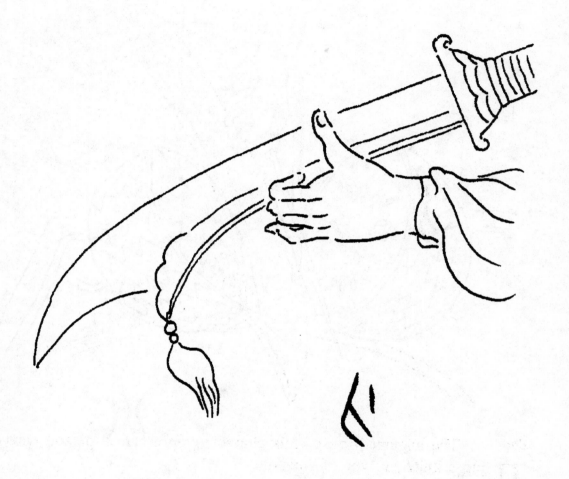

rèn

刃　　The ancient form of this character depicts a dot
being added to the edge of a knife, protruding the
position of the edge and thus the meaning.

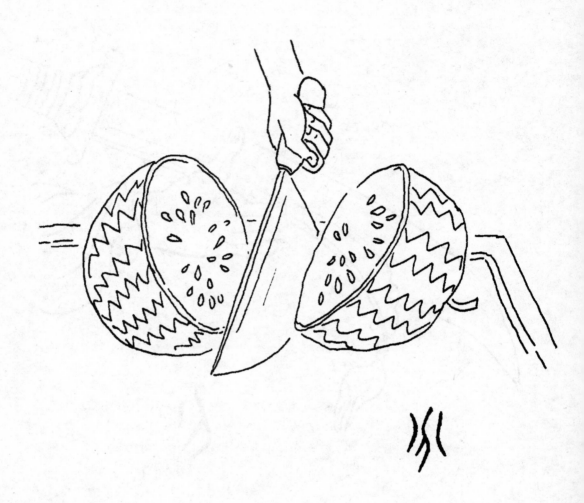

fēn

分 　The ancient form of this character depicts an object being cut into two parts, and means "分割 (fēngē: to sever)", "分开 (fēnkāi: to part)".

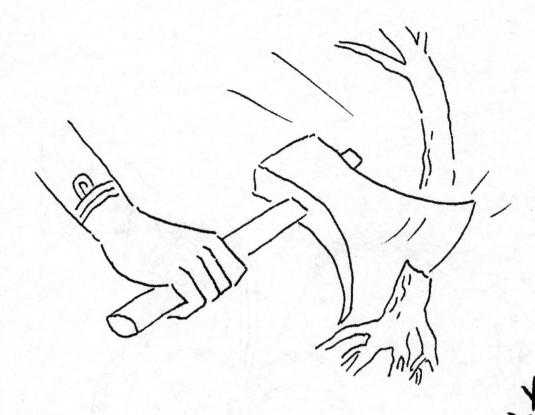

zhé

折 （斤）

The ancient form of this character depicts an axe (斤) cutting a tree and means "to break".

Han Yu, one of the eight outstanding figures of the Tang and Song Dynasties, wrote in "劝学 (*Advice on Learning*)": "锲而舍之,朽木不折。锲而不舍,金石可镂。(If an engraving is discontinued, the rotten wood will not be broken; If a carving continues, metal and stone can be engraved.)" Here the original meaning of the character is retained. According to "晋书 (*History of the Jin Dynasty*)", Tao Yuanming says: "不为五斗米折腰。(I will not bend [弯曲: wānqū] my back for five containers [*dou*] of grain.)" Here "折" represents an extension of the meaning.

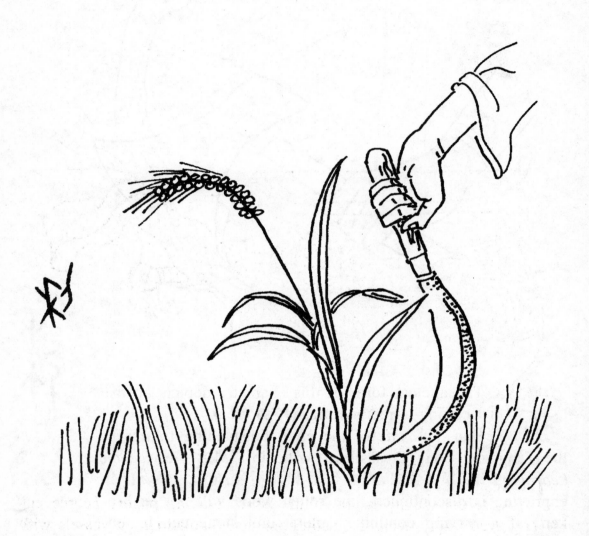

lì

利 　　This character, signifying to cut crops with a knife, means some gain after cutting. Later, the character extends its meaning to "利益（lìyì：interest，profit）" or "吉利（jílì：good luck，propitious）".

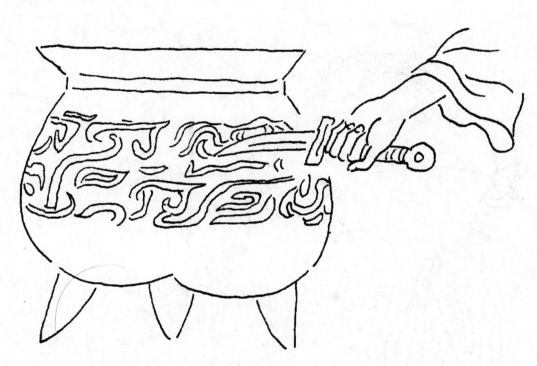

zé

则 Before the invention of the art of making paper, people engraved laws, decrees, institutions and regulations on vessels with knives. Therefore, this ancient character combines a knife and a vessel to indicate this meaning. Later, the character came to be used as a function word for grammatical purposes as continuation and transition in an essay.

The traditional form of the character is written as "則".

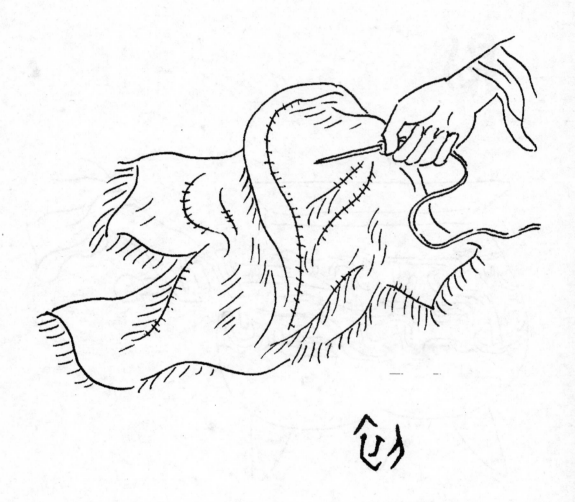

chū

初 　　　"初" was originally a title for worship. This character is formed of "衣(衤: yī)" and "刀 (dāo)", and means "to begin sewing winter clothes". In ancient times, severe winter was a hard time for the people and they paid much attention to the preparation of winter clothes. This would mean the forthcoming of winter and so the word took on the meaning "最初(zuìchū: initial)".

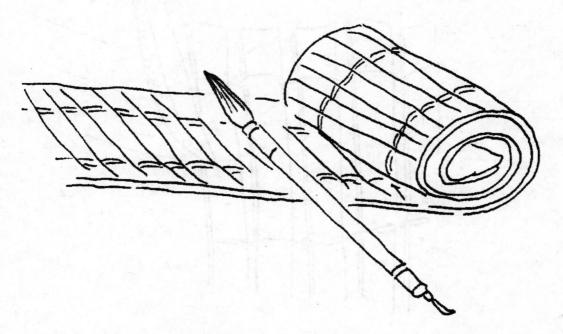

cè

册

Ancient Chinese used bamboo or wood slips for writing material. They connected with thread or leather the slips carrying characters to make scrolls. Thus, the form of this character, "册", is represented by slips connected with thread and represents what is termed "volume" by modern Chinese, as in "册子(cè·zi: book)", "史册 (shǐcè: history book)", "画册 (huàcè: picture book)". This accounts for the origination of the word "册", a measure word for books.

shān

删

Before the invention of paper, "册(cè)" or a collection of bamboo slips connected with string, was an indispensable element of people's cultural life. Thus, the creation of the "册" or scroll, was based on peeling bamboo and connecting the slips, and such an important process as to turn the raw bamboo into neatly-cut slips was termed "删". Later, the character also carries the meaning "删减(shānjiǎn：to abridge)".

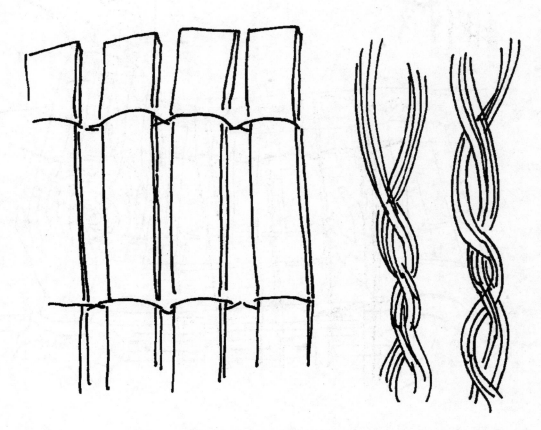

biān

编 The ancient form of this character, combining "糸(mì: thread)" and "册(cè: volume)", signifies its original meaning "to make volume or scroll with string". Later, the character extended its meaning to "编辑(biānjí: to edit)".

Later, the character combined "纟(糸)" and "扁(biǎn)", with the latter approximating the pronunciation.

455

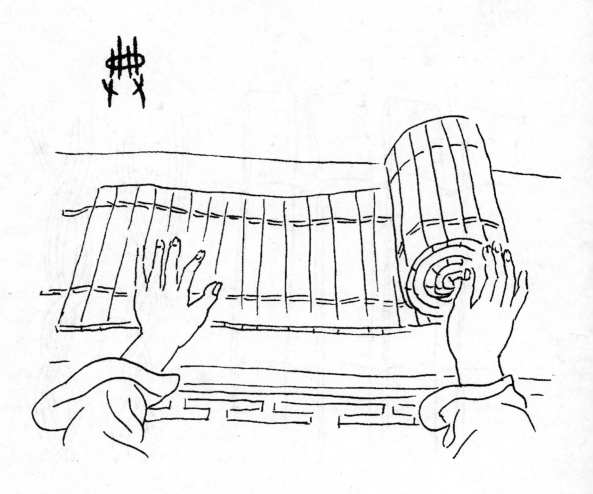

diǎn 典 The ancient form of this character, depicting two hands putting a scroll on a table, means "典籍(diǎnjí)", or "重要的文献(zhòng yào de wén xiàn：important documents)", "经典著作(jīng diǎn zhù zuò：classics)".

The idiom "数典忘祖(shǔ diǎn wàng zǔ)", meaning "to repeat classics and forget his own ancestors", retains the original meaning.

456

shǐ The ancient form of this character resembles a right hand 史 holding a vessel with scrolls inside it, signifying an official historian in charge of documents. In ancient times, such an official took on the responsibility to record emperor's words and deeds and significant events in the regime. In the Zhou Dynasty, official historians for the monarchies were appointed by the royal family and they were responsible only to the royal family for records about true events. The story about killing by Cui Shu of official historians on three occasions as recorded in "左传 (*The Zuo Commentary*)" took place in this historical background.

huà

画 The matter of first concern for emperors, especially for the first emperor of a dynasty in the conduct of their rule was how to grant land and rewards to founders and aristocrats. The ancient form of this character is drawn with a right hand holding a writing brush atop and a pair of compasses on the bottom, with "田 (tián: farmland)" added to it at a later time. It means to measure land. The form of the character happens to give a vivid expression of the practice of granting official posts and raising ranks.

The traditional character is written as "畫".

zhǒu

帚   The ancient form of this character resembles a bundle of leafy plants, meaning broom. According to legend, the broom was invented by a man named Shao Kang, or Du Kang, the inventor of wine.

fù
妇 The ancient form of this character, depicts a woman sweeping with a broom in hand. This character originally meant wife. The traditional character is written as "婦".
In modern Chinese, "妇" refers in general to married women as in "妇女(fùnǚ)".

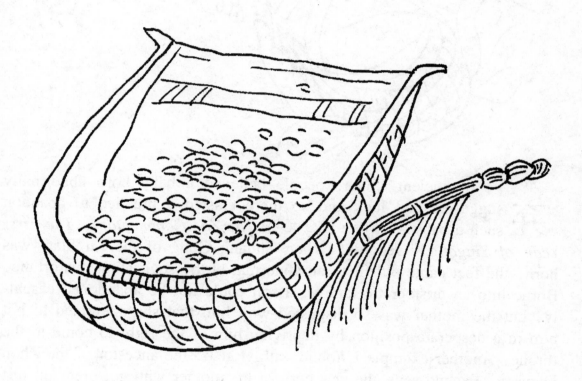

qí

其 The ancient form of this character resembles a dustpan, invented also by Shao Kang. The traditional character is written as "其" and after it is borrowed to be a function word, a "⺮" or termed "竹字头 (zhúzìtóu: bamboo head)" is added to make "箕 (jī)", indicating the original meaning.

弃   In ancient China, people believed a baby born abnormally suggested bad luck and so there existed a practice to abandon such a baby. "左传·隐公元年(*The Zuo Commentary, The First Year of Yingong*)" records: When Zhuang Gong of the Lu State was born, the feet came out first, an abnormal birth, suggesting misfortune. Borne into an aristocratic family, a son could not be abandoned casually, but the mother was so disgusted with him that she attempted to put him in a desperate position by depriving him of the right to come to the throne. Another example is found with Hou Ji, the ancestor of the Zhou Dynasty. Legend says, he was born of his mother who got pregnant just by stepping on the footmark of a huge man. So Hou Ji was named "弃" for he was once abandoned.

The ancient form of the character "弃" happens to give the expression of such a customary practice, by depicting atop a bloody baby, a dustpan in the middle and two hands on bottom, that means the baby in the dustpan was thrown away by the hands, representing what is termed "弃婴(qìyīng:abandoned child)" today.

The traditional character is written as "棄".

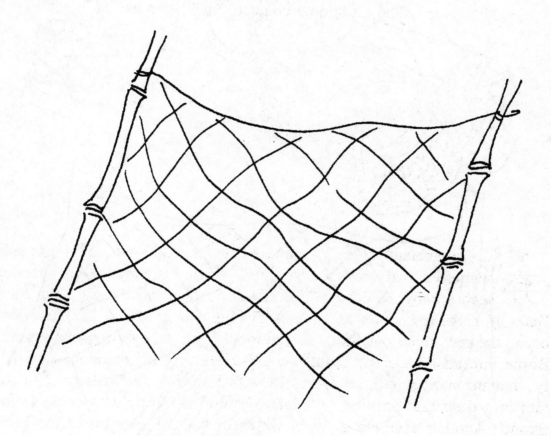

wǎng   In ancient society, "网(net)" was an indispensable tool, used
网   for hunting and fishing to secure daily necessities for food and
        clothes.

The traditional character is written as "網", and simplified to what it
was originally, "网". "网" as a component of another word can be written as "网,冈,罒,冂", indicating objects having to do with a net or trap
and punishment.

luó

罗 The ancient form of this character depicts a bird in a net, originally meaning to catch birds with a net, as in the idiom "门可罗雀(mén kě luó què：to catch sparrows on the doorway）".

The traditional character is written as "羅".

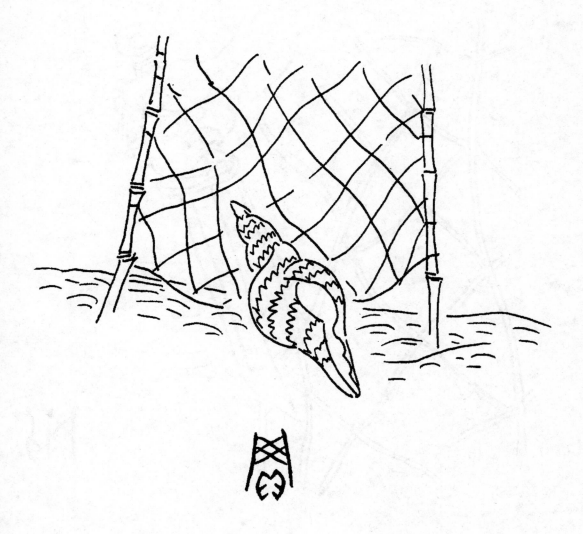

măi

买

Shellfish in a net depicts a scene from ancient life indicating at that time people paid shellfish (representing cash) in a net for what they bought, and so the original meaning is "to buy". The traditional character is written as "買".

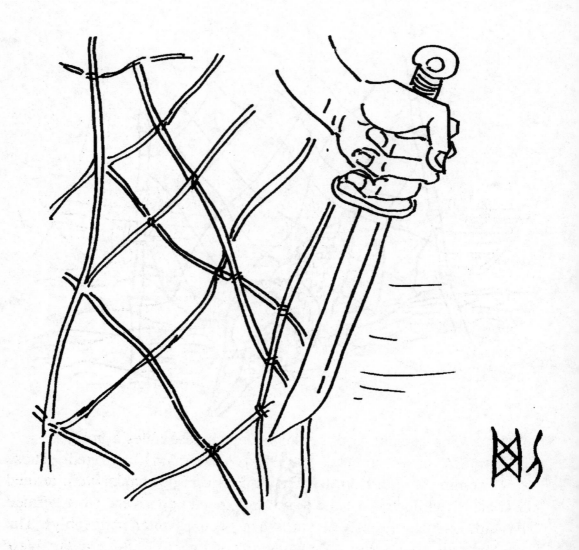

gāng   The ancient form of this character, depicting a knife cutting a
刚   net, means to cut off, and later the meaning extends to "硬
(yìng: hard)", "坚强 (jiānqiáng: firm or strong)", as in the idiom "刚直不阿 (gāng zhí bù ē: upright or to be free from flattery)".
The traditional character is written as "剛".

zhōu

舟

The ancient form of this character resembles a boat.

In ancient times, "舟" and "船(chuán)" differed. Those coming to and from the ferry docks on both banks were termed "舟(boat)" while those sailing up and down the rivers were termed "船(ship)"; later these two words can be used interchangeably. The Tang Dynasty poet, Wei Yingwu wrote in "滁州西涧(*On the West Stream of Chuzhou*)": "春潮带雨晚来急,野渡无人舟自横。(In a hurry the spring tide comes with rain in the evening, A lonely boat athwart the ferry floats at ease, but no one is in sight.)" Here the original meaning of the word is used.

"舟", as a component, often appears on the left, mostly indicating objects having to do with water and water transport.

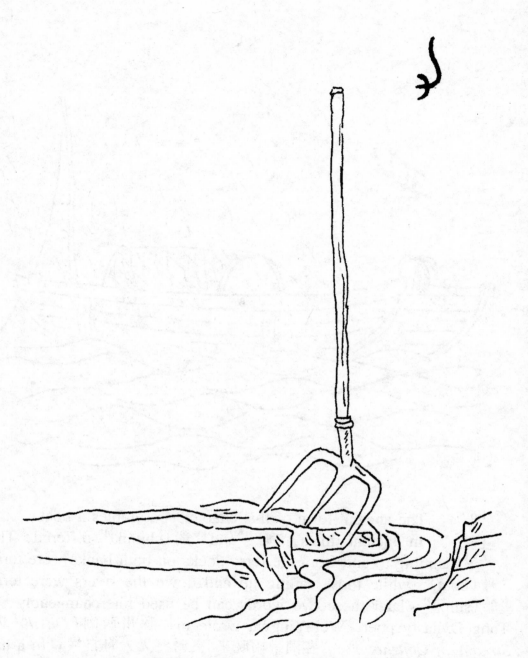

lì

力   The ancient form of this character depicts a wooden farming tool with sharp teeth, used for digging the earth. Digging requires strength and so the character takes on the same meaning as in "力量(lì·liɑng)" and "体力(tǐlì)", both meaning physical strength.

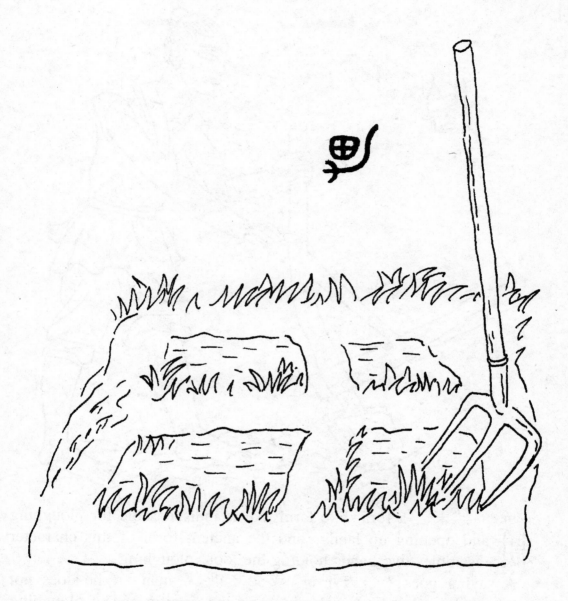

nán
男
    The ancient form of this character combines "力（lì: strength）" and "田（tián: farmland）", meaning dedication to farming, as the proverb goes: "男子力于田。(Men use their strength on the farmland.)" In agricultural society, men are the main force working on land, and so the word means men.

gēng
耕
"耒", a fork‑like farm tool is indispensable for ploughing and opening up lands, and the ancient form of this character resembles two hands holding the tool, ploughing.

A saying goes: "一夫不耕，或受之饥 (A man, if he does not plough, will go hungry)", emphasizing the significance of ploughing in an agricultural society. Sa Duci of the Yuan Dynasty wrote in his poem:"男耕女织天下平，千古万古无战争(Ploughing men and weaving women make the world peace, And for ten thousand years, war will cease)", describing an ideal society desired by the people.

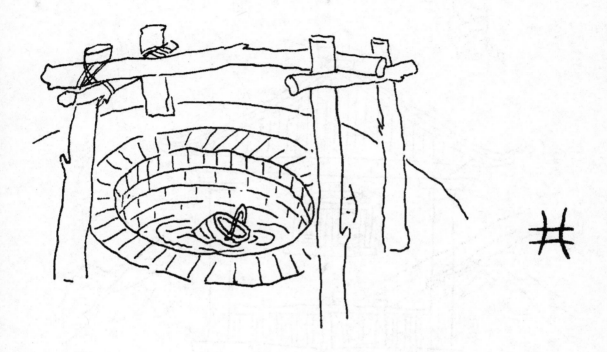

jǐng   The ancient form of this character depicts a fence around a
井 well, and in some cases with a dot inside the fence, indicating
raising water from the well.

Human life cannot be separated from water. Legend says a man
named Bo Yi invented the skill to sink a well, while Yu the Great tamed
floods. Where there is water, not only farming can be developed but also
water is available for people's lives. So people have settled down in the
vicinity of water recourses. In this sense, wells and villages share the
same meaning, which can be found in the saying "背井离乡 (bèi jǐng lí
xiāng)", describing people leaving their native town, of course, as well
as leaving the well, and in "市井 (shìjǐng)", indicating marketplaces are
set up where people gather.

miǎn   The ancient form of this character is a side view of a house, the very meaning of the character. As a component, it is written as "宀", commonly termed "宝盖头 (bǎogàitóu: protection head)", having to do with housing, lodging, the very meaning for the creation of the character.

zì

字 With a child under a "宀(miǎn)", the ancient form of this character means a child in the room. In ancient times, the single character "木(mù)" was termed "文(wén)" while the combined character "林(lín)" was termed "字". Later, they were put together and termed "文字", representing the marks, or Chinese characters, for recording the Chinese language.

In ancient times, a woman's marriage to someone was termed "字", as in "待字闺中(dài zì guī zhōng: to wait for marriage in the maiden chamber)" and "未字(wèizì: not married)".

bīn

宾

The ancient form of this character combining
"宀(miǎn)", "人(rén)", "止(zhǐ)", means the
house is visited by someone, or otherwise called
"宾客(bīnkè:guest)".

The traditional character is written as "賓".

ān
安 　After a man's marriage, a family is formed, living in peace and contentment. The ancient form of this character depicts a woman sitting on kneeled legs in room, indicating peace.

dìng

定 Living indoors is an essential demand for human life, and only after having one's own house, life is settled. The ancient form of this character depicts a "宀 (miǎn)" atop and on bottom a "正 (zhèng)" ("正" indicates "止 [zhǐ: feet]" are walking towards the position represented by "一".) and means a person has returned home safely. After all, the character means "平定 (píngdìng: peace)", "安定 (āndìng: quiet and stable)".

guǎ 　　With a man（页：yè）under "宀（miǎn）", the ancient
寡 　form of this character protrudes a lonely man, or otherwise
　　a wifeless man.

　　In ancient China, a man often introduced himself as "寡人
（guǎrén）", a polite term for a humble man. "寡人" became a
special term for emperors only after the Tang Dynasty.

huàn　　With a "臣（chén）" under a "宀（miǎn）", the ancient
宦　 form of this character indicates a laboring （obedient）
slave in a room. Obedient people may be appointed officials, and so the character refers to low rank officials. In ancient times, "官宦（guānhuàn）", two characters used together,
referred in general to officials, or public employees.

hán

寒

The form of this character portrays in the top portion a man lying on firewood in a room, protruding his exposed bare feet, which happens to coincide with the slang for "寒从脚入(hán cóng jiǎo rù：Cold comes up from the feet)". The portion on the bottom signifies ice outdoors. The ancient character means "寒冷(hánlěng：cold)".

Warm and sufficient food are basic demands for human existence. Jia Yi of the Western Han Dynasty wrote："一夫不耕,或受之饥;一女不织,或受之寒。(A man, if he does not plough, will go hungry; While a woman, if she does not weave, will suffer from cold.)"

479

宿 sù   The ancient form of this character depicts a man lying on a mattress, and means "住宿(zhùsù: to stay for the night)".

kòu

寇 The ancient form of this character depicts a hand holding a weapon（攴）breaking into the room（宀）to attack a person's head（元）, and means to infringe with weapon. In the Ming Dynasty, Qi Jiguang fought Japanese pirates（倭寇：wōkòu）in the southeast coastal areas of China. "寇" here is an extension of the meaning, referring to "来犯之敌（lái fàn zhī dí：the enemy that invade the territory）", "入侵者（rùqīnzhě：invader）".

chū   The ancient form of this character depicts a
出   foot（止）striding out of a cave dwelling and
means "出(to go out)".

gè

各 Contrary to going out, the ancient form of this character signifies a foot (止) coming into a resident place, meaning to come.

Later, "各" was borrowed to be an indicative pronoun, having nothing to do with the original meaning.

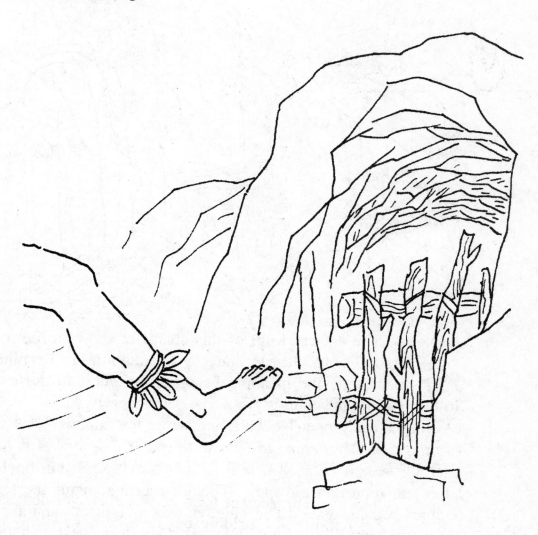

kè

客
The ancient form of this character shows a foot coming to "ㄩ(a place)" and, by an addition of "宀(miǎn)" to its top, the meaning becomes the guest in the room. So the original meaning is "客人(kè·ren: guest)".

Tang Dynasty poet He Zhizhang wrote his famous "回乡偶书 (*Jottings on My Return to Native Town*)": "少小离家老大回，乡音无改鬓毛衰。儿童相见不相识，笑问客从何处来。(In boyhood I left and return an old man, Though accent remains the same, temples became gray. The children whom I meet cannot make out who I am, With a smile they ask: My dear guest, where are you from?)"

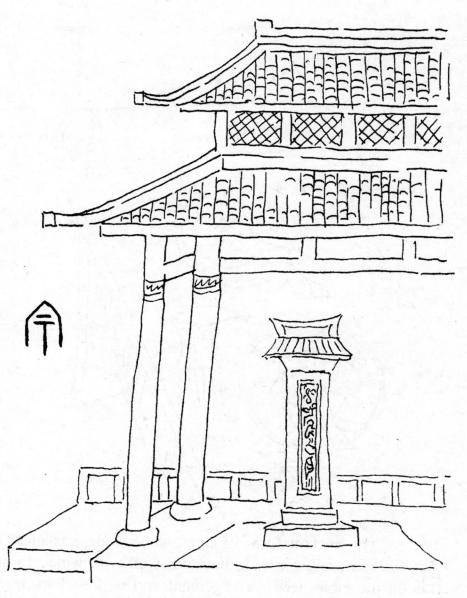

zōng

宗 The ancient form of this character combines "宀 (miǎn)" and "示 (shì)", indicating worship indoors, and means ancestor. In the idiom "万变不离其宗 (wàn biàn bù lí qí zōng: No matter how it changes, it will not deviate from its ultimate aim)", the character is used with an extended meaning of "宗旨 (zōngzhǐ: objective)", "本源 (běnyuán: origin)".

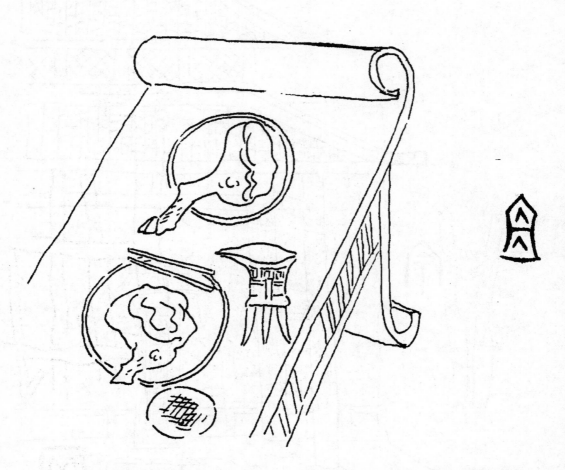

yí

宜

The ancient form of this character depicts meat dishes on the table, meaning a dish that goes well with wine. In addition, meat on the table needs arrangement and so the character also takes on the meaning of "适应(shìyìng：to be adaptable to)", "相宜(xiāngyí：to be suitable)". An example is found in a poem by Su Dongpo, entitled "饮湖上初晴后雨(*Rain Follows Sunshine When Drinking on the West Lake*)"："欲把西湖比西子,淡妆浓抹总相宜。(For symbol of the West Lake the Beauty of the West you well may take, Whether adorned with white and rose or in unpainted grace she goes.)"

láo 牢   The ancient form of this character, depicting oxen (or sheep, horses) inside a fence, means the fence used for feeding animals. The idiom "亡羊补牢 (wáng yáng bǔ láo: to mend the fence after a sheep is lost)" retains the original meaning. The meaning, "to fence animals", can be applied by extension to detaining prisoners, or today's jail houses.

zāi

灾 The ancient form of this character depicts a fire under "宀 (miǎn)", signifying a room catching fire, and thus it means a disaster.

In ancient times, floods and wild fires caused by thunder were the principal disasters encountered. For this reason, "灾" was originally written as "災" and, by combining "川 (chuān: river)" appearing atop representing water and "火 (huǒ: fire)" on bottom, indicated any disaster in general. The simplified character is written as "灾", the original form appearing in inscriptions on bone and shell.

gōng

宫 The ancient form of this character, depicts a mouth of a big cave with small caves inside it accessible to each other, representing the cave dwellings the ancestors lived in, and is a general term for all the houses. The residential houses of the royal family were termed "宫 (the imperial palace)" only after Qin Shihuang (the first emperor of the Qin Dynasty) came to the throne. The well-known "阿房宫 (ēpánggōng: E Pang Palace)" was burned down by Xiang Yu.

家　jiā

A pig under "宀 (miǎn)" indicates a pig in a room. In distant ages past, people lived a nomadic life. Later, they came to know how to feed the wild animals they caught to meet their needs for life. As they also took the animals as a symbol of their property, they came to settle down. Such families would have animals fed in their rooms. This led to the creation of the character, "家". National minorities in the southwest areas of the country still maintain the practice of feeding pigs or other animals indoors.

bǎo

宝

The ancient form of this character depicts shellfish and jade in a room, and a " 缶 (fǒu: pronounced 'bǎo' in ancient times)" was later added to provide the pronunciation. So the character means "宝物 (bǎowù: treasure)", "珍贵之物 (zhēn guì zhī wù: precious objects)".

"贝 (bèi)", as a kind of currency used by ancient Chinese, is also a type of precious object. Characters formed with "贝" indicate the important role "贝" played in ancient people's lives. Today, people still combine "宝" and "贝" to indicate valuable objects.

The traditional character is written as "寶".

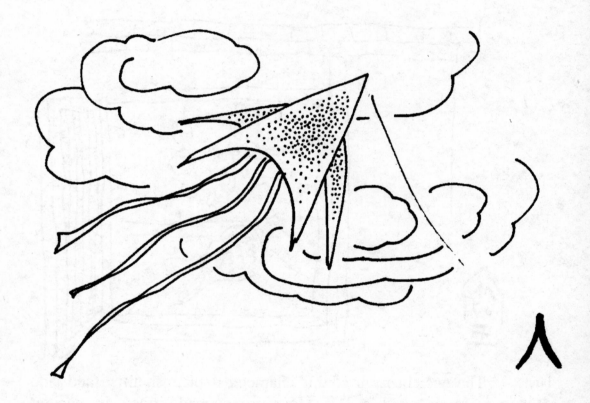

rù   With a sharp point, it is easy to thrust into another
入   object, and the ancient form of this character represents
   a sign of an entry.

nèi

内

In ancient script, the form of this character combines "冂" and "人(rén)", indicating "to enter into" a room and functions as a verb. Then, an extended meaning to indicate a position, "内(inside)" is derived from the meaning "to enter from outside".

hù   The ancient form of this character depicts a
戶 door. "户" can be used as a component, indicating objects having to do with doors.

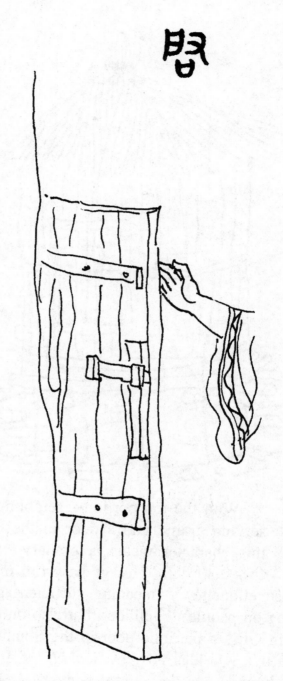

啟

qǐ

启　　The ancient form of this character depicts a hand opening a door, and means "开启 (kāiqǐ: to open)".

The traditional character is written as "啟" and simplified to its original form, "启".

cāng

仓

With the top portion resembling a roof, a container for re-serving grain, and a door in the middle, the ancient form of this character means a granary. Jia Yi of the Han Dynasty said: "仓禀实而知礼节 (A granary full of grains will cause people to practise etiquette)", meaning sufficient grain does not only have a bearing on people's livelihood but also on their morality and virtue.

Xin Qiji, a patriotic poet in the Southern Song Dynasty, wrote in "永遇乐·京口北固亭怀古 (*Thinking of Ancient Heroes in Beigu Tower at Jingkou* [*to the tune of Yong Yu Le*])": "元嘉草草,封狼居胥,赢得仓皇北顾。(His son launched in haste a northern campaign; De-feated at Mount Wolf, he shed his tears in vain.)" Here, "仓" in the quotation is used to mean "急促 (jícù) or 仓促 (cāngcù: in a hurry or in haste)".

mén

门

With a doorframe atop and two doors on the bottom, the ancient form of this character means "门(door)".

The traditional character is written as "門", and can be used as a component to indicate objects having to do with door.

wèn

问

The ancient form of this character depicting a "口 (kǒu: mouth)" in a "门 (mén: door)" means "to ask".

The traditional character is written as "問".

bì

闭 The ancient form of this character, depicting a "十" under the door, indicates "to lock the door" and the meaning is "to close".

The traditional character is written as "閉".

jiàn

间

At night, moonlight comes into the room from a gap between the doors. This character, indicating the moonlight shinning outside the door, means "间隙(jiànxì: gap)". As sunlight can also come into the room from a gap, the character can be formed with a "日(rì: sun)" to make "间".

Pronounced as "jiān" in the first tone, it appears in "时间 (shíjiān: time)" or "房间(fángjiān: room)".

The traditional character is written as "間" or "閒".

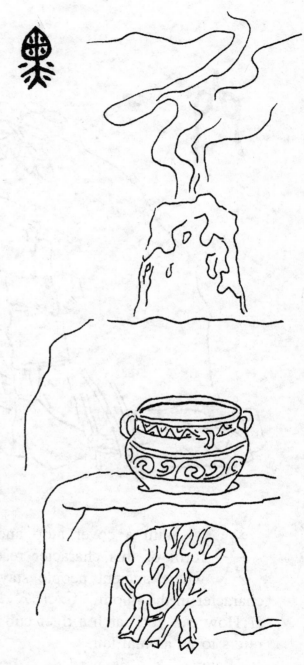

hēi

黑 The top portion of this character depicts ashes coming out from a chimney while the bottom portion resembles fire flames. The chimney becomes dark by the smoke after the fire, and so the ancient form of the character expresses darkness.

"黑" can be used as a component, indicating objects related to the color of black.

501

xuè 穴　　With a cover atop and a cave underneath, the ancient form of this character resembles a grotto or cave dwelling where ancient people stayed before they had houses. The character in the idiom "不入虎穴,焉得虎子(bù rù hǔ xuè, yān dé hǔ zǐ: How can you catch a tiger cub without entering the tiger's cave)" refers to an animal lair.

Later, "穴" is used as a component, appearing atop another character, to indicate objects having to do with a cave.

_{sǒu}
叟

At the time when ancestors lived in cave dwellings, they, usually experienced old men, used fire to discover new caves. So the ancient form of this character depicts a man holding fire in hand and means an old man. Today, in many department stores, service pledges posted up read, among others, "童叟无欺 (tóng sǒu wú qī: Neither old nor young will be prejudiced)", wherein the original meaning is used.

An old person means someone with a long period of life, and thus, an elder woman is termed "嫂 (sǎo: elder sister - in - law)"; food reserved for a long time becomes "馊 (sōu: sour)"; a person suffering from disease for long becomes "瘦 (shòu: thin)"; to keep looking for something at a place for long is "搜 (sōu: to search)".

tū

突

This character is formed with a "穴(xuè：cave)"
atop and a "犬(quǎn：dog)" on the bottom, indicating a dog suddenly rushing out of a cave, and
means "猛冲(měngchōng：to dash forwards)". "突" in the
idiom "狼奔豕突(láng bēn shǐ tū：to run like wolves and
rush like boars)" retains the original meaning.

gāo
高 The ancient form of this character depicts an observation post on a high base, and the meaning is extended to "崇高 (chónggāo: sublime)", "高大 (gāodà: great)".

The traditional character is written as "高".

háng

行 The ancient form of this character depicts a cross road and means "道路 (dàolù: road)", pronounced "háng". Walking on roads is also written as "行", pronounced as "xíng".

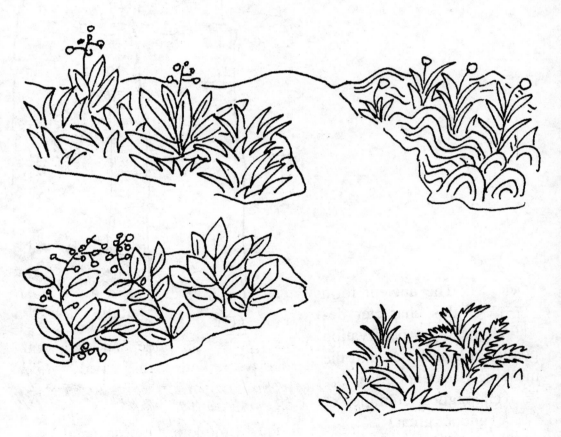

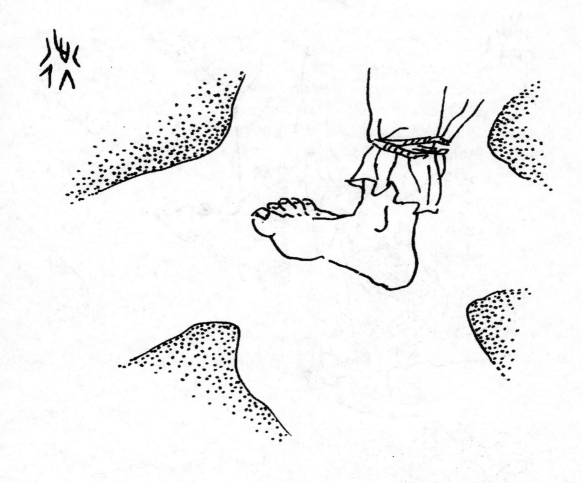

chuò

辵

" 屮 " appearing in inscriptions on bone and shell and " 彳 " appearing in seal characters, both signify road, while " 止（zhǐ）" represents feet. The ancient form of this character represents people walking on road.

" 辵 " by itself cannot be found in modern Chinese; and as a component, it is written as " 辶 ", commonly termed " 走之儿,走之旁（zǒuzhīr, zǒuzhīpáng: walking component）", indicating objects having to do with road and walk'.

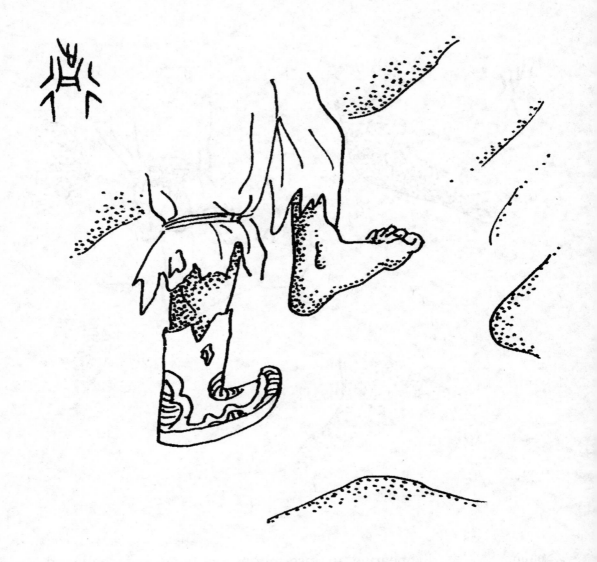

qián

前

In ancient script, this character combines the three components: "卅" representing roads leading to various directions, "屮"
representing human toes and "舟" representing shoes like boats,
to indicate that feet wearing shoes walking on roads, resulting in the
meaning "前进(qiánjìn：to advance)".

Later, the character is adopted to be a word indicating direction a-
head, and is written as "前".

dá

达 The ancient form of this character, protruding a person's feet walking on road, means " 通达 (tōngdá: to lead through, lead to)".

The traditional character is written as " 達 " and simplified to " 达 " in connection with the original intention to create the word.

nì

逆 The ancient form of this character resembles a person standing upside down, with a " 止 (zhǐ)" at the bottom and a " 彳" on the right to indicate "walking on road", and means "to come up". A man walking ahead can meet the man walking in front of him only when that man turns his steps back. So " 逆 " carries the meaning of " 方向相反 (fāng xiàng xiāng fǎn : opposite direction)".

Later, " 彳 " is changed into " 辶 ", and the character is written as " 逆 ".

510

tú
徒　The ancient form of this character signifies feet（止）walking on road（彳）, without the aid of any transport means, and thus the meaning "徒步而行(tú bù ér xíng: on foot)". From this, other meanings are derived such as "仅仅 (jǐnjǐn: only)", "白白地 (báibái·de: in vain, for nothing)", as in the idioms "家徒四壁(jiā tú sì bì: nothing but the bare walls in the house)", "徒劳无功(tú láo wú gōng: to work to no avail)".

Here in the character, "土(tǔ)" provides the pronunciation.

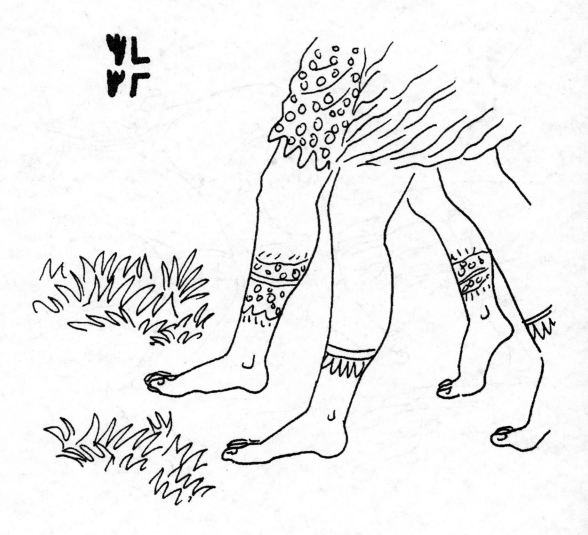

xǐ　　The ancient form of this character combines a "彳" and two
徙　feet in the same direction indicating more than one person.
　　This word is used in "迁徙 (qiānxǐ: to remove or the remove of
the entire tribe)".

In distant ages past, people throughout the world were forced to go
on expeditions because of bad environments caused by changes in nature beyond their control. This underlies the creation of the character.

hòu

后 The ancient form of this character signifies feet being tied with string on the road, indicating lagging behind because of being checked, or according to another interpretation, the string is pulled back. After all, it means "后(behind)".

The traditional character is written as "後".

xīn

辛

The ancient form of this character resembles an implement of punishment which was used when a prisoner of war underwent the punishment of being tattooed. The tattooed person must have suffered a great deal physically and mentally, and so the character also carries the meaning of "辛酸(xīnsuān：feeling miserable）".

514

qiè

妾

The ancient form of this character depicts a woman with an implement of punishment on the head, and this shows in ancient times "妾 (concubine)" was a woman slave, who was forced to marry a slave owner by his despotic power.

 zǎi
宰　　　With a guilty man beneath "宀(miǎn)", the ancient form of this character depicts a slave laboring in the house. The slaves attending to the personal lives of the slave owners were most entrusted by the owners and, if capable and experienced, could be appointed inferior officials, or termed "宰". Later, subjects who were the most powerful and granted the highest rank were termed "元宰(yuánzǎi)" or "宰相(zǎixiàng)", both meaning "prime minister".

516

zhí

执 The ancient form of this character depicts a hand-cuffed guilty man and so the original meaning is to capture a guilty man. Later, the character mostly meant "拿着(ná·zhe：to hold)", "执掌(zhízhǎng：in control)".

The traditional character is written as "執".

qiú

囚

Depicting a man being encircled or falling in a trap, the ancient form of this character means "囚禁 (qiújìn: to put in jail)". Later, the character took on the meaning of "prisoner" as in "囚犯 (qiúfàn)" or "囚徒 (qiútú)".

jīng
京 In ancient script, "京" represents lofty mountains. In distant ages past, people lived in high mountains to protect against floods. A tribe often occupied a mountain, and the chief of the tribe lived at a high and safe place. This led to the birth of "国都(guódū)" or "都城(dūchéng)", meaning "capital".

^{yì}   With a " □ " pronounced "wéi", indicating territory, and a
邑   kneeling person beneath it, the ancient form of this character indicates the area where people live together, and means " 城邑
(chéngyì: city or town)", "都邑(dūyì: capital city)".

"邑", used as a component, is written as " 阝" on the right side of another character, indicating objects having to do with names of places and
administrative regions.

wéi
韦

In the ancient form of this character, "口 (indicating capital city)" being surrounded by four feet (or two or three feet) means "围绕 (wéirào : to surround)". Later, this character came to signify "皮革 (pígé : leather)" and "口" is added to make "围", indicating the original meaning.

The traditional character is written as "韋".

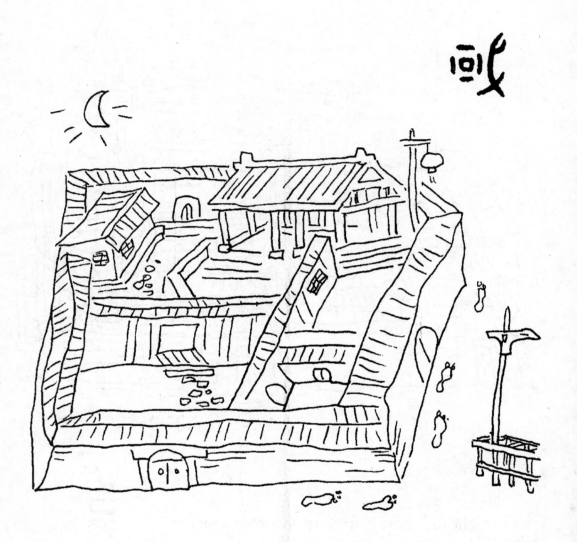

guó

国

     With men's footprints surrounding the city and a "戈(gē: an ancient weapon)" standing nearby to defend it, the ancient form of this character means "国都(guódū: capital city)", "国家(guójiā: country)".

    The traditional character is written as "或(huò)", and after it is adopted to be an indefinite pronoun, a "口" is added to make "國".

wèi
卫

In ancient script, "囗" represents city. The four footprints around it indicate a lot of people going around the city, meaning "守卫(shǒuwèi: to defend)", "保卫(bǎowèi: to guard)".

Later, the character is given "彳" to make "衛".

zhèng

正

The upper part of this character represents the capital where people live, and the lower part the feet of men. This character means "征战 (zhēngzhàn: to go to war)". Following the adoption of the character to indicate "not slanting" as in "不偏(bùpiān)" or "不斜(bùxié)", a "彳"is added to make "征" to indicate the original meaning.

According to another interpretation, with "止" going straight to the position of "口" or "·", this character means "正中(zhèngzhōng: direct to the middle)".

huí The ancient form of this character resembles a ring
回 while according to another interpretation, it resembles
a stream or river winding or flowing repeatedly.
However, it means "回绕(huírào:to go round)".

Later, the character takes on the meaning as in "来回
(láihuí:to and fro)".

kū The ancient form of this 哭 character depicts a man beating his breast and stamping his feet, indicating "嚎啕大哭(háo táo dà kū: to weep bitterly)". So it means to shed tears because of being deeply touched.

měi 每 The ancient form of this character resembles a kneeling woman, with ornamentation pinned to the hair, and the character was once used to indicate a mother. Later, the character is used to indicate "每个(měigè) or 每一(měiyī)", meaning every one or each.

gǎi

改

The ancient form of this character depicts a hand holding a whip by a kneeling boy, representing someone is educating the child to correct himself. Later, the character came to mean "correction".

méng

萌

The ancient form of this character portrays the sun and the moon among grass, indicating the time of dawn when the moon sets and the sun rises. Dawn suggests the beginning of a new day, just as grass begins to sprout. This is the very meaning of the word as in "萌芽(méngyá)".

xián

涎

The ancient form of this character depicts a man with a wide open mouth and spit dropping, causing others to drool with envy. It means spit.

The traditional form of the character is written as "次" and later rewritten as "涎", with "氵" representing the spit and "延(yán)" approximating the pronunciation.

răn

冉 The ancient form of this character depicts hair hanging downwards. Later, "髟" is added to make "髯" pronounced "rán" in the second tone, signifying a long beard. Today, man-made beards worn by actors during performance are termed "髯口 (ránkǒu)".

Later, the character is written as "冉" to indicate soft hanging willow twigs or signify the sun or the moon rising slowly.

gào   "○" being added to the mouth of an ox to prevent
告   it from eating the seedlings, the ancient form of this
character means "桎梏 (zhìgù: fetters)", "约束
(yuēshù: to bind)". Later, "木 (mù)" was added to make
"梏". Still later, the character took on the meaning "告诉
(gào·su: to inform)".

xí　　The ancient form of this character protrudes a bird's feather,
习　indicating birds about to take flight by spreading wings. Because of the repeated actions of flapping, it took on the meaning
"again and again". An example can be found in "论语(*The Analects of Confucius*)": "学而时习之(Repeat what you have learned)", wherein the original meaning is used.

The traditional form of the character is written as "習".

yīn

殷

  In the 14th century B.C., Pan Geng, the King of the Shang Dynasty was removed to a place named Yin or a small village to the northwest of today's Anyang city of Henan Province. Since then, the Shang Dynasty was called Yin in Chinese history. However, the Yin people still called themselves Shang instead of Yin.

  In ancient script, "身(shēn: the body)" represents an aristocrat with a big belly, while the ancient form of "殷 (yīn)" is formed in such a manner that the left side happens to be a "身" written reversedly, indicating the loss of their aristocratic status. On the right side is a hand holding a stick (殳 or 攴), indicating a slave. The Yin were beaten by the Zhou, and in turn, Yin aristocrats became subjects of the Zhou or their former subjects and became their slaves. This represented a shame for the Shang aristocrats and provided the historical facts which underlied the creation of the character, "殷".

POSTSCRIPT

I studied in the Chinese Department at Beijing Normal University for eight years (five years as an undergraduate and three years as a graduate). During that time as a student, my wish to be a teacher in the future solidified. However, due to all sorts of accidental mishaps, I had to leave the college even though I heartily loved campus life. It was only two years ago that I entered Beijing University. As a public official in a governmental organization, I handled public affairs every day, far from the life that I was looking forward to. So I began writing. Later, some of my books, including *Picture Within A Picture: An Illustrated Guide to the Origins of Chinese Characters*, were successively published.

I have developed a liking for linguistics and philology because the conscientious scholarship and serious working attitude of my parents have exercised on me an invisible, formative influence. They always tried to make me understand in their letters that I should establish a good foundation in Chinese and foreign languages. They said that in order to conduct foreign exchanges, especially to actively obtain academic information, mastering a foreign language is very important in modern society. After I enrolled in graduate school, my tutor, Mr. Li Dakui, introduced me to other famous professors such as Zou Xiaoli and Wang Ning who also gave me much advice during my studies in that University. Regretfully, it was not until the 1990s that I realized my dream for many years to become a teacher had been delayed. I am still conducting a study on the basic questions for Chinese characters, which is unfashionable in present society. However, I have a strong belief in this truth: How can a man who is staggering run? If a writer is not clear about the basic questions for Chinese characters, isn't it possible that his longwinded works will mislead his readers? I am willing to probe into the true essence of Chinese characters and share with readers my experience of exploration in the origins of Chinese characters.

Since the Chinese edition of this present book was published, I have found some faults and problems. The editors of **New World Press** have decided to publish this book in English edition and this gives me an opportunity to make some corrections and add supplements. Here I shall extend my thanks to them. I have carefully chosen more than 60 characters as a supplement to the original book. The Chinese characters explained by the present book are beyond five hundred. Jia Ke, who has displayed his ability in lacquer painting circles, and Shuai Mei, still a student majoring in folk arts at The Central Academy of Fine Arts, made the illustrations for the present book.

I will also extend my thanks to Zou Xiaoli and Wang Ning, the teachers who introduced me to ancient philology and from whom I learned a great deal about doing scholarly research and also conducting oneself in society.

Shi Zhengyu
Spring 1996 at Beijing University

INDEX TO CHARACTERS PHONETICIZED

541

图书在版编目（CIP）数据

汉字的故事：英文 /施正宇编著.
—北京：新世界出版社，1999.2 重印
ISBN 7－80005－332－6

Ⅰ. 汉…

Ⅱ. 施…

Ⅲ. 汉字—普及读物—英文

Ⅳ. H12

汉 字 的 故 事

施正宇　编著

＊

新世界出版社出版

（北京百万庄路 24 号）

北京外文印刷厂印刷

新华书店发行

新世界出版社发行部电话：(010)68326645

1997 年（英文）第一版　　1999 年北京第二次印刷

ISBN 7-80005-332-6

05600

9-E-3006P